GOD'
CHILDREN
IN HIS
KINGDOM

Jesus Said "Let The Children Come"

By
Charles King

This book is dedicated to:
Albert Wade, A dearly loved brother in Christ. A father of six of his own children and looked upon by many others as a father figure, especially by me. A man of Godly wisdom that was sometimes misunderstood, but always respected. A leader in the church, yet a man of humble nature. A man of the Lord who has gone on to continue his eternal life with the love of his life, Jesus Christ our Lord.

Also, to all of the children that have and still continue to pass through my life. They continue to teach me a little of the love and purpose of God for my own life and those children that are a part of the church, the body of Christ. To my wife Joyce also who is a blessing to me, that I thank my Lord every day for her presence in my life.

Introduction

And they were bringing even their babies to Him, so that he might touch them, but When the disciples saw it, they began rebuking them. But Jesus called for them, saying,

"Permit the children to come to Me, and do not hinder them, for the Kingdom of God belongs to such as these. Luke 18:16

I see this verse as a big deal, it is big, as it has so many implications. Jesus said, "do not hinder the children in coming to me." Some translations say, 'hinder.' some say. 'forbid.' In our world in this day there are many ways to hinder our children in coming to the Lord More than at any time in the history of the world. It is only going to get worse. There are so many distractions, the truth about the word of God has become something in the background. It was when I was growing up, so much more so now. Even in Christian homes.

The God of this world. The rulers and principalities of the air have made sure of that. Providing <u>stuff</u> to keep children occupied. Peer pressure, phone, electronic devices, Internet, and so much more. This is a bold statement, but I'll say it anyway. "Our children are more corrupted by the worlds influence than at any period of time in the past." And it will get worse. As technology advances, the peer pressure increases too.

Every generation for 50, 60, 70, years has grown up with more and more technological diversions, but there is so much around today it can be scary. Children having mobile phones and iPads as young as 4/5 years old. I phoned my daughter up as they were at the airport waiting to fly off on holiday to Florida, with my two grandchildren. My 4-year-old granddaughter did not want to talk to me once she realised that I was not on **Face-time**. Yes, I know that these things can be used for education, and good things. They can and are also used in a bad way.

Now I am not against technological advances. All knowledge that we acquire for these advances are God given. It is how we use it, that can be a problem. Though it does not have to be. I use the bible app, on my phone, every day to help my bible study. Writing up study notes and posting on Facebook. Also, to other social media. It is more that we allow these electronic devises to be a kind of babysitter. Something to keep the 'kids' quiet. while we get on with our adult responsibilities. It used to be just the TV, but now we have many ways to occupy our children. To do this is neglecting what is maybe our greatest responsibility to:

Train up a child in the way he should go. Proverbs 22:6

I look upon this book and what I write now as something that I am completing. This is because I started this back in the 1990 and for reasons beyond my remembrance did not finish. The leading for this now came from posting 4 short blogs entitled, 'What are we teaching our children.' Then realising that there was just too much more to talk about on his subject. Then I remembered the book that I had begun to write before. Nearly thirty years ago.

God's word does say that His gifts and callings are irrevocable.

Now what I believe more than ever is this, I know that everything that I have written about in this book can and should be applied and taught to children. God is able to use any child for the benefit of His Kingdom, just as easily as any adult. Very possibly more easily, due to the fact that they, have less prejudices, and hang ups than adults tend to have.

What I have written is applicable to adults as well as children, even though the emphasis is on what we teach our children. It is about living a Christian life, not about doing Christian things. I am not saying that the doing of Christian things is wrong but that it should be an expression of our faith and love in the Lord Jesus Christ. That it should be more than a way of life, it should <u>be</u> our life, that it should impact every area of our life; to the point that if possible, our children do not know any other way to live.

<u>That they can be in the world but not of the world.</u>

The first chapter of this book is, more or less it was written way back in 1990. I have rephrased a few things and where I have added anything It is written in italics.

Chapter 1: Children in God's Plan 1990

Has God got a plan for the children within our church fellowships or, are they just there to make up the numbers. Can we realistically expect our children to enter into and understand, all the delicate little things that go into a relationship with our heavenly Father? Then there are the worship services. Are children capable of grasping the significance of the need for reverence and awe, as we try to concentrate on our most Holy God? As we come into His presence through worship, on a Sunday morning. Will they see that the only way to get Gods attention, is by following our example? I am being a little bit sarcastic with some of these questions, yes but how far from the truth of the way a lot of adults think, is it really.

Some people may think that children are an unavoidable burden to bear in the church. Something that they must endure. Or at least for a short time until the little darlings leave the meeting and go out to the Sunday School. Apart from the few little cute ones and the babies who are good and quiet, they see children mostly as noisy, unruly, uncontrollable, irreverent. To some extent, they hold on to the old Victorian view, 'that children should be see and not heard.'

This is an attitude that is unchristian, and totally unbiblical. Could it be that this is the reason that church attendance, within the mainstream denominations has dramatically decreased over the last hundred years? It is very clear from Gods word that children are important to Him. This is enforced with warnings about the consequences of hindering the access of children to God. In Mark 10 the disciples began rebuking people for bringing children to Jesus, Jesus got a little angry with them and said, "permit the children to come." Jesus then says:

For the kingdom of God belongs to such as these. Truly I say to you, whoever does not receive the kingdom of God like a child will not enter it at *all*. Mark 10:14 -15

See to it that no one despises these little ones, for I say to you that their angels in heaven continually see the face of my Father in Heaven. Matthew 18:1

But whoever causes one of these little ones who believe in me to stumble, it would be better for him to have a Heavy millstone hung around his neck, and be drowned in the depths of the sea. Matthew 18:6

Very strong words from our Lord. So, if our children have their own angels in Heaven, in God's sanctuary, beholding the face of God; if our God delights in children this much; should not our attitude towards children within our churches, be more in line with God's?

Yes, we may find some children cute, especially the babies, but then we get annoyed when baby cries so much. So loud, that you begin to wonder why the church had to spend £5000 on a new PA system. Surely if one so small can make so much noise, then a full-grown adult should be able to manage without an amplifier.

Then there is little Freddie. A boy who every week without fail, gets up and runs back and forth at the front shouting, 'praise the Lord.' And that, just as the congregation has got into a nice quiet worshipful song. It would not be so bad, but the boy has no idea of what key everyone else is singing in! Or timing. In fact, He seems to have no musical sense at all.

And then comes dad, red faced, to try to gather up his little bundle of joy. At this point he realises that his son has been gifted with a pair of legs that would be better suited on someone like Usain Bolt. So, in comes mum to the rescue, also red faced, and frustrated, because her time of peaceful, devotional worship has been shattered.

You know what's going to happen when little Freddie is finally caught. He'll be dragged kicking and screaming, out the back to be severely reprimanded by the strong arm of justice, in a place that only his parents have seen unclothed. In your mind you realise, that is the end of the service for that family. They plan to return for next week's service, hoping that his episode will have been forgotten by then.

All this time the leaders at the front have continued in their worship as if nothing had happened. You begin to marvel at their spirituality, that the upheaval, that has just taken place had not seemed to interfere, with their communication with the Heavenly Father. While you may have been thinking that if, parents cannot keep their children under control, maybe they should tie them down, or better still not bother bringing the children at all.

It cannot be right, that these overactive little darlings, should be able to disrupt, and spoil our time of 'adult' worship. Would it not be better if Sunday School started at the same time as the 'adult' service, and lasted just as long as the 'adult' service? That way we would see the little treasures until the informal tea and fellowship time. Then they can run about and make noise as much as they want. Within reason!

This is a bit exaggerated I know, but how far is it from the attitudes of some adults have I really strayed? That is a question that you can answer for yourselves. From experience I do know that this kind of attitude does exist amongst the adult population of the Christian family, to varying degrees. I agree that parents should be able to control their offspring to some degree.

So, what is God's attitude towards children? How does He view them; where on His list of priorities does He place children? How can children play a vital role in the life of the church? Can God really use these young ones to the benefit of His kingdom; His church; His people; the world? These are good, and pertinent questions, of which I hope to give some answers to in this book.

So, we have already seen that God has delegated angels to represent each of our children that constantly behold gods face. Worshiping and looking to God on the children's behalf. Jesus said.

"Permit the children to come to me; do not hinder them; for the kingdom of God belongs to such as these." Mark 10:14

Jesus goes on to say'

"Whoever does not receive the kingdom of God like a child shall not enter it at all." Mark 10:15

Just from these just from these two verses, it is clear, that apart from adults being an example to children. Children are an example to adults, in what is possibly one of the most important aspects of the Christian faith. That is receiving the kingdom of God. You cannot get in unless you become as a child, receive it like a child.

Incredible? Not to God. It is not through intellect, Maturity, works, or anything else. It is through the simple faith as a child has.

Let's get back to little Freddie. Now I am not advocating that a forty-year-old person should get up and run up and down in front of the church, shouting at the top of his voice, 'Praise the Lord.' I mean, you would think he was crazy or something. Especially at the point where the worship had become quiet and reflective. Then again, if God had just done something in his heart, or he got healed of a terminal disease, and that was the only way that he could express the way he feels; it could be that everyone else is out of tune with God. Apply this thought to little Freddy.

Maybe the reason that little Freddie did what he did is, because God had touched him in some way or spoken to him. Would it be better to find out why he seems to be throwing the service into disruption? I tell you that if the reason is because of something that God has done or said to him; and that something is not shared with the whole congregation; the people that are in the meeting will be missing out on something marvelous. Something that the whole church could be rejoicing over. Something that the whole church needs to hear in order to advance   into Gods presence.

Now little Freddie has been dragged screaming, and kicking out of the service, has been denied the opportunity to be a possible witness to the grace of God. The opportunity for God to really pour out His blessing on that gathering of His people has been denied. And, you know what most people will go home from that meeting, feeling that they had not really Met with God, or of not having a sense of the presence of the almighty God.

It had been just another normal, run of the mill service. Nothing's changed, nothing new. Just what most people had expected, and those who had expected more, they have gone home feeling that there was something missing. At least they had worshipped God, despite how they felt.

I invented this scenario, with little Freddie, for an example. Deep in my heart, I know that it is too close to the truth. The truth about the way some adults view children in the church. My heart burns, and I break down in tears at the thought. The thought that we could ever treat our children with such disregard, concerning the things of God. Spiritual things not intellectual things. The thought is this, If I can feel this way so strongly, how must our heavenly Father feel? If my heart can be broken in this small way, how much more is God's heartbroken? What is Gods attitude towards children? Well Jesus put it very simply.

"Whoever causes one of these little ones who believe in Me to stumble, it is better for him to have a heavy millstone be hung around his neck, and to be drowned in the depth of the sea." Matthew 18:6

You can't argue with that; it is very clear. This statement is recorded in three of the gospels. Which serves as a reminder to how important, and how impressed the disciples were by Jesus attitude towards children.

On another occasion Jesus rebuked the disciples, for hindering the children coming to Him. The disciples were stopping parents from bring the children to Jesus, that He might touch them. Hindrance can come in many forms. Just thinking that a child will not understand what being born again is all about, is hindrance. And so, for our attitude to come in line with God's attitude towards children, it needs not just an outward action, but an inner change of heart. A renewing of the mind.

I am convinced that children have an important role to play within our churches. A church without any children in it, is a dying church, regretfully there are a few of those around.

There are some churches that have a thriving children's work, yet they are still dying. This is because the children's work is kept separate from the normal everyday life of the fellowship of the church. The only time that they mingle, is at a monthly or bi-monthly 'family service.'

The children hardly know any of the adults in the church, and the adults know the children equally as well. A lot of the time this can be, because a good number of the children in the Sunday School come from families that don't attend the church, maybe except for the occasional family service.

Now I am not decrying the work that these children's workers are doing in the Sunday Schools, many are called of God for this purpose. Nor am I ever going to criticize the provision of Sunday schools that are open to children of people that do not attend church. It may be the only time that these children get to hear Christian teaching and influence.

My prayer is for a blessing upon all those Christian children's workers, who I know sometimes spend hours in preparation, to teach and reach children with the living word of God. Why do I pray a blessing on them? For the same reason that I have spent the last thirteen years teaching children about the love of God. Because they, as I do have a love of God for children.

The point that I am trying to make is this. The lack of children from the everyday life of the church, means that the church is lacking something vital to the life of that church. In the same way, a church that consisted of only children, would be inadequate to sustain any life or growth, towards being the living organism that God intended the church to be.

It would be wrong of me, or anyone to declare a death warrant on any churches like the above example; for that would deny the great and marvelous work that God has done, in raising some of them up to begin with. This through men and women of vision. It is not Gods desire that any church should be without children, or that adults should have their meeting, while the children meet somewhere else.

An added note here – I have been in many churches where it seems that parents take things to occupy the children during the worship, until they go out to Sunday School. Where they may or may not have a 'children's' worship session! Do you think that this is right in God's eyes? Worship should be for all, to help them come into the presence of God.

On the day that Jesus cast out the buyers and sellers; and turned over the tables and seats of the money changers; in the courts of the Temple; the chief priests and the scribes grumbled, because the children were crying out, "Hosanna to the Son of David." Then Jesus reminded the Priests and the scribes what it said in the Psalms. He put it this way.

'Out of the mouths of infants and nursing babes, thou (God) has ordained praise.' Psalms 8:2

I have, as I write this, upon my bedroom wall a card; from one of the children in my class on a Sunday. It says, 'Dear Charlie, thank you for the work you do as the Glorie company leader. (this what we called our children's work), and we used the official Glorie Company Materials. I am glad that you are serving God as a leader in our church family. Signed ....

Now I have to say that this means more to me than any praise or compliment, that I have ever received from any adult within our fellowship. It is a wonderful feeling that comes, when various children, at different times, come and give me a hug. Or even just to spend a little time with me talking. I am glad that I am not the only adult within our fellowship that receives this kind of attention. God must feel really great when so many children begin to pay Him attention, *to have a real relationship with Him,* to worship and praise Him.

Children are a gift from God. Through children we are blessed of God. Children are the fruit of the womb; they are a reward. They bring joy into our lives. Having received two such gifts for myself, I get amazed sometimes just how great a blessing they are to me. Their names are Dawn, and Benjamin. They cause me anguish sometimes, but I have so much love for them; I cannot be angry at them; I get more frustrated at them than angry. When they have done something wrong, and I had to chastise them, it is not long before I find myself having to tell them that they are forgiven. *It is within minutes.*

We have a God with a bigger heart than yours or mine. He has more love for His children, (all adults and children), than I will ever have for my children. So, with the special place He has in His heart for children, you can begin to understand why He says, 'It would be better for you to have a millstone hung around your neck and be drowned in the depths of the sea, than cause one of these little ones, who believe in me, to stumble.'

To see the worth that children are to the Kingdom of God/Heaven, you just have to look at their worth through What God says in His word. Yet there is still more. You may say that children are the church of the future, but the truth is, that the children are the church of today.

This idea that children are the church of the future, needs to be eradicated from our minds. Yes, they may be the leaders of the future church. But they are still the church of today. They always will be. I tell you, the children that are the church of the future are those who have not been born yet.

God in His word says of our children who are believers, *after talking about testing the spirits, and warning about the spirit of the antichrist, John goes on to say this:*

'You are from God, little children, and have overcome them, because greater is He that is in you, than he that is in the world. 1 John 4:4

You see that God has already adopted them as His sons and daughters. God has already made them to be our brothers and sisters in Christ. Their sins are forgiven just as much as any adult believer. *Even future sins.* John says in chapter 2 of the same letter,

"I am writing to you little children, because your sins are forgiven, for His names sake. 1 John 2:12

This is the only time we read in the New Testament, that sins are forgiven for the sake of the name of the Lord. You can see that it is towards little children that it is directed. Thinking about this. I came up with this thought.

The almighty God, who created everything, including man, could have easily devised a way that humans could be recreated, birthed full grown, and fully developed. *He created Adam from the earth full grown, He did not create Adam as a baby.* God did not make it that way, the order He set was that offspring would begin life as babies. Growing, developing learning from parents and everything around them.

My mind at the time of writing this, can only conclude that, our God desired for us to experience the enormous blessing that children would bring. That we would experience at least some of joy, in our children, that God has for us. *Watching us grow spiritually, gaining wisdom from the things that we go through.*

There is a whole lesson of its own in that. How we rush to the aid of a child, that we have just seen fall head long onto the hard concrete path. God has more concern for His children than we could ever have, or imagine. God is so concerned for us, that when Jesus returned to Heaven, He did not just leave us to get on with His work, all alone. He sent His Holy Spirit to help us.

The same Spirit that descended upon Jesus in the form of a dove: The same Spirit that empowered Jesus and worked through Him. This is the same Spirit, that our Father in Heaven has given to us. Given to empower us and enable us to do the work that He has called for us to do. *To continue where Jesus left off.* To help us to be everything that God had planned for our lives.

This gift of the Holy Spirit is for you, and your Children. Acts 2:39

There is not one level of Christian life for children, and another for adults, who are supposedly mature enough to handle the deeper things of God. I tell you from experience, a lot of the time, children are more able to handle the deeper things of God than many adults. Simply because they receive them like children. On the other hand, adults receive them like adults and complicate them. *Many adults try to use intellectual reasoning to try to work out what the bible says. When it is just a matter of applying faith.*

Just there, that is where the worth of children to the Kingdom of God begins. We ought to look and watch our children much more. There is so much more that we can learn from our children, about the Kingdom of God. More than we able to imagine. In Matthew 11, Jesus prays and gives praise to the Father, because He hid things of Spiritual value, from the 'wise and intelligent.' God was please to reveal them to babes.

God is no respecter of persons. If he gives gifts to adults for the furtherance of His Kingdom, he can also give them to children for the same purpose.

Every good thing bestowed, every perfect gift is from above, coming down from The Father of lights, with whom there is no variation, or shifting shadow. James 1:17

Children's worth to the Kingdom of God is immeasurable. If there is a long running debate within your church, that remains unsolved, it maybe be a good idea to ask a child what God has to say about it. You may find the solution that you are looking for. Children are a part of the body of Christ, just as much as any adult. We need to take 1 Corinthians 12 seriously *when we think about the worth of children to the body of Christ.*

God has placed the members, each one of the them, in the body, just as He desired. 1 Corinthians 12:18

We may cringe at the thought of asking a child advice on some important matter to the church, but God, yes God, is ready to give more honor to those parts of His body that we see as not a lot of use. Even when it comes to the successful administration of the church.

Scripture does say that we should test prophesy, *Not just prophesy but also knowledge and wisdom,* and this is what should be done. The way to do this is this instance would be to seek the Lord further, *and you may come to scripture that just says, 'go preach the gospel, heal the sick, raise the dead.'*

What you should not do is give the poor child a third degree, on how he is walking with the Lord; what his prayer life is like; or whether he reads the bible every day; or even if he knows what the voice of the Lord sounds like! My friends, this would only at best cause the child, to question his faith. At worst it could destroy his faith altogether.

On the other hand, seeking the Lord for confirmation, and receiving it, would greatly improve your appreciation of the value of children to the Kingdom of God. It would also build up the faith of the child. The child in turn, would also have more respect for the adults in the church.

To hear what God has spoken through a child, and then to question that child's validity to speak out the words that God has given him, or even worse do nothing, could cause that child years of turmoil *in his faith.* In fact, he may never gain the courage to speak out again. *That would be a great shame. A waste of the gifting's of God. It would be like taking God's gifts and trampling them under foot.*

I remember at the age of twenty-two, I received a word of prophesy, and being a young shy Christian, of less than 3 years, I had a fear. The fear of coming to the elders of the church with the things that God had shown me, to those people that I considered greatly more mature in the Christian faith. I sought God on what I should do. God sent me to a Minister in the next town about 10 miles away.

A minister of the same church denomination. This man Spirit filled, understanding, and sympathetic. He instructed me on the correct way to go about presenting this word that I had received, to my church leadership. This I did, just as he instructed.

A couple of weeks later, I was asked to come before the church deacons. I was questioned quite intensely. At the time I thought to myself, why are they doing this to me? Why are we not just praying and seeking God as to what we should do about this word from God?

They were questioning my validity to be someone through which God might speak. I left there feeling that although God had been there supporting me, holding me, and strengthening me My confidence in these men as leaders of God's church had gone. A very sad position to be in.

There was one of the deacons who was wise enough to ask questions that would establish the word was from God. His name was Albert wade the man I have dedicated this book to. Albert went on to become a great friend and brother in the Lord. He left this earth to continue his eternal life in 2018. A man, who will be greatly missed.

Our attitudes must change towards one another as brothers, and sisters in Christ. We must begin to see each other as God sees us. When this sort of thing is normally said, we normally only associate it as adults to adults. If there is one area in which our attitudes need to change more than anywhere else; it is towards the children that believe on the Lord Jesus Christ.

We need to change the way we see their worth to the Kingdom of God; to our churches; to the Christian faith that we claim to hold so dear. Without children among us our churches would eventually die.

We need children as much as we need leaders. They are an essential to the Christian faith. *Children are an essential part of the body of Christ, the church.* In my heart I feel, know, that without children there is no real Christianity. *Put it another way Christianity is nothing, almost meaningless without children.*

One of the aims of my life, is to learn all I can about God, from children, *and their perspective.* This I am not ashamed to say, even after working for over twelve years teaching the things of God to children. If we all took time to learn just a little about the Kingdom of God from children, then I am sure our faith would become much stronger.

I am writing to you, little children, because your sins are forgiven for His name sake. I am writing to you, fathers, because you know Him who has been from the beginning. I am writing to you, young men, because you have overcome the evil one, I have

written to you, children, because you know the Father. 1 John 2:12-13

Chapter 2: Jesus v's Father Christmas

What are we teaching our children?

I was writing a post for Facebook, on what are we teaching our children. There came to be too many things coming into my mind on this, that I had to write a completely new post. The title of the new post the pt. 1 of 4 posts, was the title of this chapter. Jesus vs Father Christmas.

It is not really a competition between the two, but more of a challenge about what we actually teach our children that is true, against something that is a lie. I was thinking about all the things that we tell our children that are actually lies. Things like this; 'father christmas won't come unless you are good, He knows if you have been naughty or nice.'

This is just wrong. At best it shows that this imaginary person is someone who is ready to judge the child. At worst it can cause an unhealthy, and unbiblical fear of judgement. The Verse of scripture I was using is,

Train up a child in the way he should go, even when he is old, he will not depart from it. Proverbs 22:6

This verse takes me back nearly forty years, when I was called by God to work with children. Teaching in the Baptist Sunday school, working with traditional Sunday school materials. They were perfectly good materials, which worked well.

There seemed to me though, to be something missing while using them. It was kind of teaching the stories without application. Teaching principles without effect. Teaching **religion,** rather than practicing the life of God working through the children. Teaching the way without the life. That means the truth is missing. Only a half truth is a lie! ... .

You have to think about that one for a minute. That is why if you have to go to court and give testimony, they make you swear to tell the truth, the **whole** truth, and nothing but the truth.

I was a young Christian, having become born again less than a year before. I knew the difference that accepting Jesus Christ as my Savior had made in my life. In the back of my mind the thought was, 'how come no one told me, that I needed to accept Jesus as Savior before.

Why was it not explained to me, or anyone who went to the same church of England Sunday school, that we cannot be acceptable to God unless we are born again? Why were we not told, that being good, praying, reading the bible, and trusting that works (being good) will not get us into heaven when we die.

If we had been taught the truth of the word, why Jesus came and died. At least we would have had the right information to make a decision. Either to accept Jesus or reject Him. Why had I been hindered for so long, in this way? From seeing that God wanted me to come to Him through Jesus. Is that someone else trying to make a decision on my behalf, about what I can or cannot understand?

I did not want to be like that towards the children that I was teaching in Sunday school. I wanted all the children that I taught to know the way, the truth, and the life.

God showed to me then, that children are as important to the kingdom of God, as any adult. Jesus was sacrificed once for all sin. The sin of the whole world. The sin that we even have not yet committed. Once for all people, once for all time. He died for the sin of the whole world. He died 2000 years ago.

Not just for the sin of that generation, but for our sin in this age too. Yours and mine, also our children. All sin is forgiven. Everybody has a right to make a choice to accept or reject the grace of God, and His forgiveness.

For the death that He died, He died to sin once for all; but the life that He lives He lives to God Romans 6:10

There are a few scriptures that refer to Jesus sacrifice once for all. I know that different people interpret these differently, according to circumstances, or doctrine. But the truth is All means All, it does not matter if you believe it means all sin, for all people, or for all time, they all apply. I don't want to list them all, but just see here what Peter says.

For Christ also died for sins once for all, the just for the unjust, so that He might bring us (*all*) to God, having been put to death in the flesh, but made alive in the Spirit. 1 Peter 3:18

Everyone's sin is forgiven. Jesus said it is finished. At that point His sacrifice was enough to allow all to come to God. All sin is forgiven, even a little child or baby. You may say, "but a baby has not had a chance to commit any sin yet, but the bible says that we are born into sin. That means we are born as sinners.

The fact that everyone's sin has been forgiven just has to be recognised and accepted. Jesus died to forgive *all* sin. That is every sin that is in the world, even before it is thought of. There is a verse of scripture that indicates that children are sanctified by at least having one parent who is a believer.

For the unbelieving husband is sanctified through his wife, and the Unbelieving wife is sanctified through her believing husband: for otherwise your children are unclean, but now they are holy.
1 Corinthians 7:14

That does not mean that we should not teach children about the grace of God through Jesus Christ. We should be telling them that they are Holy, Speaking the word of God over them. Children begin to learn to speak by hearing people around them speak. From the moment of birth. We talk to them.

That is substance going into their brains for processing. These days we are even told that we should talk to unborn children in the womb. They can be learning the truth of God's word even before they can speak.

You may say that what I am saying is a bit farfetched, but it is true that babies are constantly learning, from everything around them. What they see and hear, smell and feel. That is just physical things, we cannot understand the possibilities of spiritual things.

The Holy Spirit can teach your child things before they can talk, or reason. If they learn the truth, see the truth demonstrated in their parents lives, and are a part of living the truth, they will become the truth, in what they think, say, ... and act.

As Living stones being built up as a spiritual house.
1 Peter 2:5

Children have the need and right to know Jesus just as much as we do as adults. That they may be built up into the spiritual house. Timothy learned as a child 2 Timothy 3:15.

Samuel was a child when He first heard the voice of God, having been raised with a priest in God's service. God made Solomon king as a child.

Jeremiah was, (in his own words), just a youth when god spoke to him. Solomon was still a child when he became king over Israel. God asked him, What can I give to you, Solomon asked for wisdom, and he got it. As a child. So much wisdom that people were amazed. God can speak to and use even young children.

Jesus had to learn as a child. He had to learn to walk, talk, eat, go to the toilet. Just as we all do. He was a child, that had to experience growing up exactly the same as other children around Him. He had to learn to read and learn the scriptures just as we do.

Think about it God in the flesh as a child, it says that he grew in wisdom and the grace of God, then after His extended stay in Jerusalem at the age of 12, it says that,

He continued to grow in wisdom and stature, in favor with god and men. Luke 2:40-52.

Who did Jesus learn from? It does not say, but obviously his Godly parents, and Godly relatives, and with help from the Holy Spirit. This is just the same as how we learn from reading or hearing the word of God. The Holy Spirit illuminates, or quickens something we read, to us.

Jesus learned the same as every other child of his time. It is just that His focus was on His father in heaven, His word, and fulfilling His purpose. Jesus did not begin His ministry until He was 30 years old. Until then He worked as a carpenter. At thirty years old is not when He got the revelation of His purpose, of who He was. Most probably before He was even 12 years old, He Knew.

When do you begin training your children? Babies get hungry and cry, so you go feed them, very quickly they learn that when they cry, you go and attend to them. So, they start crying just to have you attend to them and not just for feeding. They begin to learn from birth, and they learn some things fast! Especially how to get your attention.

As they grow, they learn that they cannot get everything they want and need by using the same methods, so they adapt. They learn new things to do, new ways to coerce you to giving; not only what they need, but also what they want.

We teach our growing children many things, even before we think that they are able to understand. Even just by watching us they learn. We talk to them, so they learn our language. We sing to them, and pull funny faces, trying to get them to smile. We do many things that teach them that they are loved, comforted, protected by us. This from the time of birth until maybe our death.

We never stop teaching, even when they get to the point of being able to teach us a few things. The truth about this is that we teach bad things as well as good things. A question to ask is, When do we begin to teach them the truth of the gospel, and what Jesus has done for us? When they are old enough to understand?

No that is much too late. The life of Jesus should be evident in our everyday life, so it becomes a learning process for children even before they can walk or talk. They should grow seeing us pray, read the bible, living a life led by the Holy Spirit. As I said before, reading, and declaring the word of God over them.

Jesus vs father christmas

We teach little children about father christmas, and the Easter bunny. These are lies. At least we should teach them the truth about St Nicholas, and the association with the myth of father christmas. Instead of making father Christmas into a God like person.

We teach our children that Father christmas is a magical person, who rides a magic sleigh, pulled by magical reindeer. That he can get to every house in the world, down the chimney, to deliver presents in one night. This is a lie of massive proportions. You can't call it anything else.

We tell children that if they are not good that father christmas will not come. We encourage children to write to father christmas to tell him what they want him to bring for them. This is all lies, fabrications that have nothing to do with truth. It corrupts the truth, and the view of the truth.

It is against God and the reason that he sent His Son. I would go as far as to say that father christmas is a type of Antichrist. I know that is strong statement, and that a lot of people will call me a killjoy. But we are teaching children a lie; teaching them that it is OK to lie; and teach their children, yet to be born children to lie.

It has been said to me that I should not spoil the

mystery of father christmas for young children. This to allow the lie of father christmas to become more real to our children than the truth of Jesus. The gift that God gave to us all. That cannot be right.

If you think that I am a killjoy or are one who thinks this way about what I am saying, you are one that says to me that I should spoil the truth of the birth of Jesus, and the wonderful things that God did to bring about the birth of Himself come as human flesh. The wonderful gift from God to allow us to have eternal life. Which is a real and close relationship Him. This to allow the lie of father christmas to become more real to our children than the truth of what God gave.

What is wrong with the truth about Christmas? It is OK to tell children the story of father christmas, read them the poem that started all of this fantasy. It is only a fairy-tale, a story, that is it, let children know that it only a story. The truth about Jesus is also a story, but not just that, it is an historical fact. A fact of what the almighty God did, so we can have a relationship with Him.

For God so loved the world, that He gave His only begotten Son, that whoever believes in Him shall not perish but have eternal life. John 3:16

Further on in John chapter 17, Jesus explains what eternal life is. Not something to look forward to in the future. Not an after-death experience. It is something to have now and forever. Not just when we get to heaven, but right here and now as we live this earthly physical life. We have eternal life right now. It is a gift from God to you and your children and as many that are far off who will believe.

And this is eternal life, that they may know Thee,

the only true God, and Jesus Christ whom Thou haste sent. John 17:3

Eternal life is a relationship with God, and Jesus. Our Children have a relationship with us from the day of their birth, and through us they, from that day begin to have a relationship with Jesus. The deepness of the relationship children develop with Jesus, will depend on the depth of our relationship with Him. We can teach children to develop their own relationship to a deeper level.

Teach them to have an independent relationship with the Lord. This should be a natural normal part of raising children. We should be teaching children that God, through Jesus Christ, wants a personal relationship with them. That it is as real as the relationship that they have with us. This begins with teaching the reality of God, Jesus, and the Holy Spirit.

The biggest problem is that as adults, our relationship with the Lord is not as strong or as deep as it ought to be. We are not seeking first the Kingdom of God. We do not put enough emphasis on our own relationship with the Lord. Life and dealing with it's complexities becomes a priority. Our relationship with God should be our first Priority.

If we make our relationship with God our first priority, then our children will learn the importance of having a relationship with God. If you put your relationship with God first, they will see this and think that it is the normal thing to do. They will want to do as you do.

Going back to Christmas, and some of the things that we do.

Christmas trees

Something that most see is an essential to the season. It seems like they have become a seasonal Idol. They mark the beginning of the season. Christmas begins when the Christmas tree goes up! We spend a few hours setting it up, with decorations and lights, candy canes, and maybe foil covered chocolates, then we marvel at the work of our hands.

I can here you are thinking or saying, "Oh no there is no way Christmas trees are an idol." You may be right, or you could be wrong. Then we wrap up presents and place them under the tree. This is almost like putting them on the altar of an idol as an offering.

Yes, I am pushing the thought, maybe over top. We even put a star or an angel on the top, this kind of makes it look more Christian. Then on Christmas morning we sit around the alter of the tree while the presents are dished out.

The truth is that when Christmas comes around it takes over normal logical thoughts and actions. Even unbelievers will go to church on a Christmas morning. With the attitude of once that is out of the way we can then, worship at the Christmas tree, then worship the TV, before the Dinner, Then more worship of the TV. All the time the Christmas tree twinkles in the corner reminding you that it is still there.

It is essential that the lights are kept on all through the Christmas season, as long as there is someone in the house, until bedtime. It is not really an idol?

What are the origins of the Christmas trees. It was thought of as pagan tradition in America in particular, brought over by Europeans, it was a German tradition. There are several stories. One about Martin Luther setting up candles on a pine tree outside, near to his house.

Another is about a Benedictine monk, Boniface, confronting some native Germans performing sacrifices before an oak tree. Oak trees being sacred to the god Thor. The monk set to chopping the tree down, in order to stop the worship of false gods. The legend says that a fir tree grew out of the fallen oak tree.

So, the fir tree was adopted as a symbol of Christ. Being triangular in shape, it was decided the each of the three points represented one part of the Holy Trinity. This is just religious idolatry. We make the tree Christian by placing a star or an angel on top. It is like having a picture, or a carving, or any other depiction of Jesus on the Cross; or even an empty cross; and people going and kneeling before them to pray. It is religious idolatry. So much of what we do for Christmas is much the same.

Holly and ivy, mistletoe

The use of these plants goes back to at least two hundred years before Jesus. Used by Druids to decorate their homes at the coming of winter. The reasons were for fertility and supposed healing power of the plants.

Adopted by Christians and changed the thoughts about them, saying that the fact of them being evergreen, the same reason for having a Christmas tree is related to the everlasting life in Jesus. Making them again a religious icon, a kind of idol. Pagan idols or rituals made Christian just by reasoning, not by the truth of God's word.

The fertility side of it is where we get the kissing

under the mistletoe. So, basically a husband and wife who kiss under the mistletoe will become fertile enough to bear a child in the coming year. An old pagan tradition, which is simply worship of plants.

Christmas day

Even Christmas day, I am not against it. I think it is good to have a day to remember the day that God gave his Son to the world. The truth about Christmas day is this. It is not the day of the year, that Jesus was born. I think that most of us understand this.

The reason this date was set to remember Jesus birth is this. At some point the leaders of the Church in Rome felt that Christianity was in process of dying out. This because of the strength of the faith of people in ancient gods, Idols.

They had festivals for their idols on or around the 25th of December. So the leaders of the church in Rome declared that we should celebrate the birth of Jesus on that date, to rival the celebrations of the ancient idols. Not because Jesus was born on that day. Just to raise the profile of Christianity Amongst the general population. To pay more attention to Jesus, rather than the other gods. It had nothing to do with trying to convert people to Christianity, more to set up Jesus as a rival.

Father Christmas

I think that most of us know that there is a connection between St. Nicholas and Father Christmas. In case you don't here is a brief summary of who St Nicholas was. He was a Bishop who in the fourth century AD, lived in what is now called Turkey. He was very rich, and a very kind man. He had a reputation for helping the poor and giving secret gifts to those in need, and notably in the regards to welfare of children.

Because of his kindness, he was made the patron saint of children. He is also the patron saint of sailors. The reasons for this sound more like myths than truth. We get the name Santa Claus from, the Dutch name for St Nicholas, 'Sinterklaas'.

The myth of Father Christmas came from the 1822 poem by Clement C. Moore, A Visit from St Nicholas, that was later published entitled, The Night Before Christmas.

Late in the 1800's Father Christmas became visualised by Thomas Nast, who drew thousands of pictures, that made a lasting visual impression. It was a magazine, Harpers weekly that suggested that Santa lived in the North Pole. He did not get a red suit until 1931 in a Coca Cola advertising campaign.

Christmas stockings

The story goes, that there was a widowed man with three daughters. He was having a tough time financially and did not have enough money to give as a dowry for them so they could get married. Also, his pride would not allow himself to accept any kind of charity. St Nicholas heard of the man's plight, wanted to help. So, one night he slid down the chimney of their house, and filled the stockings of the girls which were hung up to dry, with gold coins.

Another version tells that he threw the golden balls through an open window, and they landed in the stockings. This is partly where the giving of presents comes in. Although, it is also a part of pagan traditions for the festivals the took place at this time of year. Then it was adopted by the Christian church, and that the giving of presents is really supposed to in some way represent and acknowledge the gift that God gave to Us. We give because God gave to us the greatest gift that He could have. His Son.

All of these things are just stuff that has been picked and adopted by the religion of Christianity. They have become symbols/icons of Christmas. To be really Spiritual they have become idols. They have nothing to do with the truth of what happened, or what it meant when God sent His Son.

The truth is so much more amazing anyway. God became a man! Let's look at it a bit deeper, into the truth. It is a story about prophesy, angels, virgin birth, and Joy to the world. About truth. Hundreds of years before, God spoke to Isaiah about this. And there are many references to Gods plan of redemption way before Isaiah, and also after.

Therefore, the Lord Himself will give you a sign: Behold, a virgin will be with child and bear a son, and she will call His name Immanuel. Isaiah 7:14

Immanuel means God with us. God humbled Himself and took on a human body. He was born as a baby, real flesh and blood, He was human. That is amazing in itself. The creator of heaven and earth, of all that is in the earth. Our creator came down and experienced what is like for us to be born and grow.

He had to learn to walk, and talk, and feed Himself, even how to control His bowels. Jesus was a real person, not just a fairy tale or myth. The King of Kings and Lord of Lords was born in a stable, with animals round about and straw. The Saviour of the world could not find a proper bed for His mother to give birth. A very humble entrance into this world.

About nine months before this Mary had a visit from the Angel Gabriel to let her know what was going to happen to her. A young teenage girl already engaged to be married was going to become pregnant by the Holy Spirit. That seems to be an awesome thing. I can't imagine what Mary felt, or was thinking.

There must have been thoughts about, what will the neighbors think, the family think, what will my fiancée think. We know she was worried about what Joseph would think, because she asked the angel, who basically said, don't worry I'll go tell him.

Then there were the shepherds, who must have been scared out their pants, A whole host of angels. (I wonder why nobody else saw or even heard the noise? I am sure they did not sing quietly.) Why were the shepherds the only ones to get told the amazing news about Jesus the Messiah? Were they the only ones around found to be worthy enough to hear of this good news?

Guess what, they walked out on the job to go see the 'wonderful sight.' They knew that the sheep would be OK to leave. Here's another truth about the birth of Jesus, the shepherds were the only ones to go see the baby Jesus in the stable in Bethlehem, on the day of His birth.

The wise men came up to two years later. It does not say that there were three of them, just that they brought thee different gifts. They went to king Herod to ask where He was. Herod did not know, so he ask the scribes, to find out where the messiah was to be born. they went to Bethlehem and could not find Jesus.

They found Jesus in Nazareth. Probably walking by now. After this Herod's decree went out to kill all baby boys under two years old. So, the angel told Joseph and Mary to go live in Egypt. More, hundreds of years old prophesy fulfilled. You see, some truly amazing things happened the life of Jesus.

These things are real, not mystical, not just stories to make us have a happy moment for a few days. The truth that will set us free to live an eternal life. This not as a future hope, it is for living in the here and now. A life free of sickness, free of the consequences of sin, full of the love of God. A life to live in the power of the Holy Spirit flowing out from within us. An abundant life, full of joy, and peace no matter the trials we may have to go through. These are some of the things I believe we should be teaching our children. Things that I will cover in the chapters to come.

I see that there is not so much of a competition, more of a battle to fight for the minds of our children. This is not just about the fantasy of christmas, but about much more; about the things that we teach children. It's not really just about, Jesus Vs Father christmas, it is more about the truth Verses a lie.

Ask yourself, is it better to teach our children to accept a lie or accept the truth? I am trusting, hoping that you said the truth We don't wish for our children to grow up as liars, so why do we lie to them. They learn from us. They will copy us, our good habits as well as the bad ones.

As I said earlier they begin the learning process from the day of birth. Actually, it is long before that, as they are affected by a mothers emotions and moods while still in the womb. A mothers emotions and moods can be affected by her husband, and any other person they may be around. As a child grows every little lie they hear, and then understand that it was a lie, enforces a false truth, that is actually OK to lie.

I call it a false truth, because to a developing mind the lie becomes the truth. Then later they read what the bible says about lying, and a conflict is raised within the mind, and the heart. Believe the bible or my parents. This is a possibility, it does happen.

Lying can also open a door into a person's mind to the devil or demonic influences, for them to come in and corrupt a person's way of thinking. You accept lying to your children, maybe to other People, then when the devil, comes and whispers a lie to you, and you receive it. This a problem for us all, especially when not walking in the Spirit. The bible tells us that:

If we walk in the Spirit, we will not carry out the desires of the flesh Galatians 5:16

That is to allow the Holy Spirit, to lead you in your walk with the Lord. Just think, if we taught our children these truths, how would their lives turn out to be? How much more equipped would they be, to deal with situations and problems that come up in their lives? If we teach them that the Spirit of the living God is alive inside of them, that this Spirit will help them whenever they need it.

That all they need to do is pray and ask for wisdom, and trust, and allow the Spirit from within them to lead them in the way they should go. Give them the right words to say. Above all we should be teaching the word of God, it is real. It is alive and active. **Could it be that, by not teaching our children the truth of the word of God, we are hindering them in coming to Jesus.**

But Jesus called for them, saying, "Permit the children to come to Me, and do not hinder them, for the kingdom of God belongs to such as these.
Luke 18:16

By not teaching our children, that if they become born again, and be baptised in the Spirit, letting them know that the Spirit is a gift from God to help them in their daily lives, we are hindering them in coming to Jesus. Telling children that they have to wait till they are old enough to understand what it all means, is a lie.

Tell them the truth, let them decide. Allow the Holy Spirit to guide and teach them. Jesus called the Holy Spirit by several names. I like the name 'The Helper,' because it is a description of what He does, and what we should allow Him to do all the time. Wouldn't you want the Holy Spirit to help your Children to grow up right? Live in the knowledge and power of the Holy Spirit.

I did not know any of the things about the working of the Holy Spirit in a person's life, when I was a child. I didn't even know about having to be born again; before I was acceptable in the eyes of God, to be able to come to Him and know that My prayers would be answered. I was not taught any of this truth. Saying nothing, not teaching the truth is lying. There is such a thing that is recognised in law as lying by omission. This is not telling the whole truth, or not saying something that could be relevant to the truth.

We should be helping our children to come to the knowledge of what Jesus has done. It is actually more than that, we have an obligation in the lord to make sure that our children are taught all the truth. Not just what we think is appropriate for their age. Yes, some things you may say can be age related as to the ability to understand.

Teaching does not only come through words, but also by actions. The way we live demonstrates more than just telling a child how to be. It teaches them the right or the wrong way to conduct their lives. Don't forget the Holy Spirit can give your children understanding just as much as He can for us, as adults.

But some may say, "you have faith and I have works; show me your faith without work, and I will show you my faith by my works. James 2:18

To say or assume that a child cannot understand things, is to undermine the work of the Holy Spirit. Think about it, we read the bible sometimes and we do not get any glimmer of what it is talking about. Yet another time when we read, the words seem to come alive to us. That is the Holy Spirit. He can do the same for your children.

Jesus verses father christmas, is a non-contest, but only if you think in this way. Jesus has been given the Name that is above every name. That at the name of Jesus every knee shall bow, even father christmas.

We should, as Christians, be teaching our children the truth about Christmas, Only the truth. Not mixed with the lies and myths surrounding father christmas, presents, christmas trees and the like. These things only go to water down the truth and power of the gospel. They are teachings and doctrines of men. Doctrines of demons.

Yes, I said it, things designed to divert us away from the truth. If you accept and give place to these things you are at best undermining the gift of God. At worse negating and replacing the truth with a lie.

But the Spirit explicitly says that in later times some will fall away from the faith, paying attention to deceitful spirits and doctrines of demons.
1 Timothy4:1

For they exchanged the truth for a lie, and worshipped and served the creature rather than the creator, who is blessed forever. Amen
Romans 1:25

Don't you see that Father Christmas, and reindeers are creatures, Presents have become idols. As have christmas trees and decorations. People light up their houses and the whole street with multitudes of lights just to bring a bit of festive spirit. It is nothing compared to the glory that God has set before us in His creation. God said to Abraham, "look at the stars, Look at the sand. So shall your descendants be." This is being fulfilled through Jesus. The one who was born. The reason it is called Christmas.

Chapter 3:
How And Why? The Pointless Questions!

How and why can be two eternally unanswerable questions. Sometimes it does not even matter about the answers. I am sure you have heard a child ask, Why? When something has been told to them. They get to a point in their mental development, that they have begun to want a reason for what you tell them. Could be something that they should not do or say, or even, this is what we should do or say.

The question comes, Why? You give them your best answer, and they come back at you, Why? So, you explain a little deeper, and they come back, but why? There is no answer to end all whys. How? Is just about the same. They can become pointless questions. You just have to have faith and believe. But Why? How?

Being Born Again

This is, or can be a delicate, debatable subject among adults, let alone when talking about children. Back in the late seventies, and eighties, after I was born again, it was common for born again Christians to ask new people they met, if they were born again. Even to people who were Christians. I was asked several times when going into a different church, or the Christian bookstore. Nobody though asked me if I was baptised in the Spirit, that I can remember, until several years later. Being born again, and baptised in the Spirit, are two of the foundational required aspects of the Christian faith.

First is being born again. You cannot get to heaven unless you are born again. Next is the baptism in the Holy Spirit. You can get to heaven without the baptism in the Spirit, but you will not be able to live the victorious abundant life that is a promise of God. A promise for this life, not just in heaven.

Anyway, the reason for this being born again, being a debatable subject, is that many people who attend church can be offended by talk of being born again. After all they have been faithfully going to church all their lives. They believe in God or they would not be going to church. The Devil believes and knows that God is real, more than most of us do. God's word says that he knows and trembles. The devil has seen God, he was an angel in heaven.

There are people who live a good life, obey the Ten Commandments, they have a good heart, and try to help people as much as they can. They are full of love that flows out of them, and they care about people. They will say or think, **"What has being born again got to do with my religion?"** They think that they are doing what God wants for their lives. Doing things. Though they ignore the very basic principle for being a part of the Kingdom of God. Listen, you can keep all of the commandments, not just the ten, and it will not get you to heaven!

Jesus said to Nicodemus, **"Truly, truly, I say unto you, unless one is born again he cannot see the kingdom of God." John 3:3**

Nicodemus did not understand, and he was a Pharisee, a ruler, a teacher of the Jews. We know what it means, it is explained to us, as Jesus went on to explain it to Nicodemus. Not everyone though, understands or accepts this teaching. Maybe because we grew up or were taught religion, and not the truth. Maybe because it is too complicated for our minds to understand the implications. We don't need to, we do not need to understand it all, just believe. Accept the truth of Jesus' words and be born again.

It is a Spiritual birth. It does not matter why or how; you just have to have faith in what Jesus said and believe. Why would anyone resist this. Jesus says it plain and simple. It is just accepting Jesus as Savior. I have known plenty of people that say, 'But it is how you live your life and treat people that counts.' Yes, that comes into it all, but you still cannot get into the Kingdom of god without being born again.

It does not say whether Nicodemus understood or accepted what Jesus was saying. The fact remains that it is a foundational truth, we must be born of water, and of the Spirit. It is a mystery of God how this happens. For me it was just a realisation of the truth, that God wants to save every person on this earth. A realisation that there was something more than just trying to live a good life, being good to people. Trying to live in peace with everyone. Trying to obey the law.

Not doing stupid things. I had done some stupid things. A realisation that it did not matter what I had done or said, that God loved me, and still wanted a relationship with me. A realisation that all I had to do was accept that Jesus was my savior and be born again. I did not work it out. It did not take any reasoning on my part. I just knew that it was the right thing to do.

I did not understand it all. I did not know how it was going to work out in my life. I did not know about God wanting to use me for the His Kingdom. Knew nothing of the way Gods power flows through people. All I know was that it was like a light came on in my understanding as far as God wanting a relationship with me. Being born again is not an intellectual experience, it is a

Spiritual experience. It does not happen independent of us though; we have to agree with what the Spirit is showing us. It is a Spiritual rebirth. I did not even know the truth about baptism until after I started reading my bible.

I don't think anyone understands fully what the implications are, when we make the choice to accept Jesus as our Savior. So why do expect children to come to an age that they can understand. As I have said, being born again is a Spiritual experience not an intellectual experience. Some adults that have a knowledge of the bible will probably have some revelation of the things they have read in the past. It is like a turning on in their understanding. That is good, it is of benefit to them.

It is like this. We are born of water; this is the physical birth. We don't need to understand what is going on before we are born It just happens when the time is right. It is the same with the Spiritual rebirth, we do not need any understanding except that it is time to allow it to come to pass. When we are physically born, our mother knows that the time has come for us to be delivered physically. When we are reborn Spiritually, our Heavenly Father knows that it is time for us to be delivered spiritually. It is a work that God does, not out of our human thoughts, it is a Spirit to spirit communication.

We cannot begin to develop Spiritually until we have been born again. We can learn and know all the religious traditions of men that there are. Gain all the knowledge, and worldly wisdom that goes with the knowledge. Spiritual wisdom and knowledge begins with Spiritual rebirth. We are born again as Spiritual babies. We have to let go of worldly ideas of what we think is Christianity and begin to learn what Gods ideas and plans for us are. For some this can be a hard thing to do, having so much religious belief and doctrine instilled in us. For a child it is so much easier, because they do not have all of the religious junk stored up in their minds.

In real life some children seem to develop more quickly in some areas than others. No one is the same. Some children learn to talk sooner than others. Some learn to read more quickly or write. Some are more artistic than others. Some learn practical skills quicker and more easily, than other children. Many times, it is working out what they are good at and putting more focus on that thing at the expense of other skills.

It is pretty much the same with Spiritual rebirth. We grow and mature at different rates. Some choose to walk a path that seems the easiest. And shy away from things that seem to difficult or need more concentration than we are willing to give. We think we will get there in the end, using natural talent and abilities.

The fact is, we are taking the long way around, yes God is still with us, but we took the detour. When we do this, we are using the worlds way of thinking to get us to a Spiritual target. Trouble is that we expect our children to do the same. This is using intellect to reach a Spiritual maturity.

Jesus answered and said to Nicodemus, "Truly, truly, I say unto you, unless one is born again he cannot see the kingdom of God." John 3:3

No one can get to heaven; no one can have a living relationship with the living God; no one can really understand the Spiritual things of god, unless they are born again. It is the truth, the way that God has set as the rule, in having a relationship with Him. You can get to know about God intellectually, but you cannot know God intellectually. You can only get to know God through the Spirit.

It begins with Spiritual rebirth, being born again. That is God's plan for every human being. No matter what age. Jesus died for all sin, for everybody on this earth. God had to become a physical human in Jesus to reconcile physical humans to Himself.

All have sinned and fallen short of the glory of God Romans 3:23

There is none righteous, not even one Romans 3:10

How much of the bible do you believe, it is the word of God. It is all true. God speaks to those who belong to Him, even if they are not listening. Nearly every time I read from His word. I see something that God is saying to me. I admit, I am not always listening, but I am getting better as each day passes. Sometimes I cannot get to sleep because God is talking to me so much, showing me things, teaching me things through His Holy Spirit, I have to sit up and write them down. God Has never stopped talking. The world in general, have stopped listening. Even born-again Christians, sad to say. God has so much to teach us.

To get to the point of what I am trying to say. Being Born again is a Spiritual experience and not an intellectual one. What happens when we are born again is this. God takes our sin stained spirit and replaces it with a brand-new spirit. The Holy spirit comes and seals our brand-new reborn spirit. Why? So, our reborn spirit cannot be infected by sin any longer.

See, it is a Spiritual thing that happens. Yes, we must accept, and agree to this. Why? God set a law in place that He will not violate. He gave us free will, the ability to choose. We can say yes to the leading of the Spirit, or we can say no. If we say no, we cannot get to know God in a personal way, we cannot get to know the kingdom of God.

How does this happen? We do not know. We draw near to God, and He draws near to us. I have explained what spiritual rebirth is to some degree, but there is infinitely more to it than what I have said. It is a thing that God has ordained, and He works it through His Spirit. We as adults, don't fully understand even after our rebirth.

Why do we think that children need to understand it, before they become born again. We have to go through Spiritual growth. Why can't children go through the same experience. Jesus told us that we should have faith as a child. If God can replace our spirit with a new one, then He can do the same for any child.

How it happens, Only God knows. Why it happens the way it does, that's Gods business. Why would we dare to question it. These are pointless questions. The Holy Spirit can come into a child and seal his spirit just and easily as an adults. We have to stop thinking on behalf of children and give them the opportunity to receive Jesus as their Savior. Or, are we going to reject God's word on behalf of another person? In this we have no rights.

Yes, how and why are pointless questions when it comes to understanding the workings of the Spirit in someone's life. No matter how old or young they may be. It is a mystery, how God works, but His mysteries are revealed as He works. They are revealed through His works. The fact is this, we have to understand the basic principle that every person needs to be born again to enter the Kingdom of God.

You do not need to understand why God has set things up in this way. You do not need to understand how it happens. You just have to believe God and accept it. It is God's word for everyone. The most marvelous thing is this, that the Kingdom of God is placed within us. If we allow, for where the Lord reigns there is the Kingdom of God.

Neither shall they say, Lo here! Or, Lo there! For behold, the kingdom of God is within you.
Luke 17:21

Chapter 4: Baptism In Water

Water baptism for some reason can be a touchy subject. I know that as a baby I was Christened. But that is not baptism. I know this, because when I became born again I had the desire from the Holy Spirit to get myself baptised. I did not know why I had this desire. I just knew that it was something that I had to do. Before I became a Christian, I thought that I was a Christian already.

After being born again, I realised that I had not been a Christian at all. I read in my bible that Christians are people that are born again and then baptised. I had been Christened, but now I understood that that did not make me a Christian. I used to go to church occasionally and now I realised that did not make me a Christian. I even used to challenge people who used God's name in vain, that did not make me a Christian.

There are many stories of baptism in the New Testament, all believed, repented and were then baptised. You have to believe the truth before you can repent. Some are baptised in the Holy Spirit before baptism in water; but you cannot be baptised in the Spirit until you accept Jesus as your Savior.

The Word of God clearly says, 'Repent and be baptised.' The religious practice of infant baptism, I will cover in the next chapter; Whether you believe in it or not is up to you. I am not trying to condemn, just enlighten to the truth of the bible. You read that:

Peter said repent and be baptised, in the name of Jesus Christ for the forgiveness of your sins, and you will receive the gift of the Holy Spirit. Acts 2:38

The Greek word Baptizo is where we get the baptism from, Means immerse. The Hebrew word Mikveh means an immersion. This quite literally total immersion. That is why in biblical times the baptism of people was done in rivers; both by John the Baptist, and Jesus and the disciples. John the Baptist was baptising at Aenon 'because there was much water.'

Why did they do it in the rivers if they were not going to totally immerse them. They could have just carried a pitcher of water around with them, to pour on people's heads. But they didn't. They immersed people. Christening is not baptism. It is a religious doctrine of men, and became a substitute, for real baptism. The bible says repent and be baptised. It is plain and simple, you cannot be baptised until you repent, until you become born again.

It has become a custom within churches that practice baptism, to have candidates go through a series of lessons, before they are baptised. This is so you can understand what baptism is about and why that church practices baptism. This is not a bad thing. It is good that the church wants you to understand, what baptism is, and what it means. Though I don't think it should be a requirement. Most of what can be included is related specific to church membership of that particular church or denomination, and what the church expects from you being a member. Some which are direct biblical truths, some are not. Things that are like club rules.

The important things about baptism can be shared within ten to fifteen minutes. They are normally spoken about in the baptismal service. They did not have time to run baptismal classes in the early church, it was not done at all in the bible. Nowhere do you read anything about teaching people about what baptism is all about, separate from the preaching of the gospel.

Again, it just says believe and be baptised. Many times, we can at worst negate the work of the Holy Spirit within a person who has repented and wants to be baptised, because that is what the Spirit is leading the person to do. At best we water down, weaken the work that the Holy Spirit is doing within the person's life.

As I said everything that a person needs to know about baptism can be shared in less than 15 minutes, yet there are some churches that require attendance at baptismal classes for an hour at a time over several weeks. The biblical way was to baptise people straight away, at their conversion, (rebirth).

Also, something that should not be a requirement, is the membership of any particular church organization. I remember going to baptism classes because it was a requirement. They would not baptise me unless I went to the classes. I also remember that there was a lot of things within those classes that were not necessary, and some things that I did not agree with, that were not biblical. By this I mean they were more to do with the religious concepts of men than biblical concepts. If someone believes (they are born again), they should be able to be baptised, whatever church they go to. When you are baptised you are not baptised into membership any particular church. You are baptised into the body of Christ; which is the Church.

On the day of Pentecost, the word of god was preached, in many languages. Then peter got up and preached, most probably in Hebrew, that people should repent and be born again. They were then baptised in water that day. Three thousand were added to their number. Where were the pre-baptism lessons? It would have taken weeks. But then the spread of the gospel might well have had to stop, while they taught three thousand people what it means to be baptised. No, that is not how it worked. It worked because of the work of the Holy Spirit. Believe, repent and be baptised.

When I was just twenty years old, and member of my local Baptist church, (I had only been a Christian for about a year), there was a members meeting. On the agenda was a request from a young fifteen-year-old girl for baptism. This girl had become a good friend of mine and had helped me some in understanding my faith. She had encouraged and helped me to learn to play the guitar, so I could lead the Sunday School children in worship.

Anyway, she was a member of the Congregational church in the town, membership of that church was a requirement for being involved with the young peoples uniformed group of that church. The congregational church did not baptise, or even have the facilities to perform baptisms.

During the Baptist members meeting I could not believe the discussion that they had about baptising this girl. Some were totally against it because she was a member of another church. Some were saying that they don't think that she was old enough to understand about baptism. Most of the people there were deacons of the church. Most of the people at the meeting Knew the girl as she came to most of the Sunday evening services. But they could not agree that it was the right thing to do to baptise this girl.

I stood up for her and said that nothing of what they were talking about matters. The girl believes in the Lord. She has been born again. She cannot get baptised in the Congregational church. You know her. You know her heart is for the Lord. We are a Baptist church. That is what we believe, we baptise people. There should be no argument. Let's just do what the name of our church says and baptise her. What I said cut through almost all the arguments, but we voted and all, but a couple said yes to the girls request to be baptised.

If we teach our children, the about truth about Jesus. That He died for our sin. That He wants us to believe in this, and Him. That they have to accept Jesus as their Saviour, to be born again. When they do become born again, at whatever age. Then they come to us and asked to be baptised, we should not question it or them. They come having been led by The Holy Spirit to know that they need to be baptised.

To question them would be to question the wisdom of God. Also, to question them would be to question their faith. Why would you do such a thing? The Spirit works His work within His people. In any case, if you have taught them all the other things about coming to the Lord, then you should have been teaching them that they need to be baptised also.

I saw a video on Facebook, of a boy about six or seven years old being baptised. He was in the water with the Minister, who was talking too much. By the time the Minister got to the point of saying in the name of Father, the boy had baptised himself, ducking under the water. It was quite funny to watch.

In the bible they did not have time to give a mini sermon for each person they baptised, it was just, "I baptise you in the name of Jesus." If with your mouth you confess that Jesus is Lord and believe in your heart that god raised him from the dead, you have the right to be baptised. No questions asked. It is a divine right, as a child of the living God.

Guess what? It does not matter what age they could be four or five years old they could be one hundred and five years old. As the Spirit leads a person. The truth is that the need for baptism should be part of the preaching of the gospel. Not something that is added on afterwards.

There was a time in early church history, that people would put off being baptised, until they were on their death bed. This was because of a wrong teaching. The wrong teaching was that if after you believe and were baptised, if you sinned there was no way to be redeemed a second time. That would as it says in **Hebrews 6:6** to crucify Jesus again.

It was a fear that if they made a mistake and sinned, they would not be able to get back into a right standing with God. I am sure that there were those also, that loved their life of sin, that they just put of accepting Jesus, thinking that they could do it on their death bed.

I have come across people like this. They say, "I am not ready to commit my life to the Lord yet." Or they will use some other excuse. The reality is that they don't really believe. Why would a person neglect a so great salvation? The Lord says, "believe and be baptised!"

The Symbolism Of baptisms

The symbolism of baptism is important. The first thing about it is this. It is a declaration of your faith in the Lord Jesus Christ. By being baptised you are saying that you know that Jesus died for your sin, and you believe and have accepted that. You are declaring this in the company of witnesses. You are making a confession of faith in the Lord Jesus Christ. Romans Say's this:

"If confess with your mouth that Jesus is Lord, and believe in your heart that God raised Him from the dead You will be saved." Romans 10:9

Though it is not actually necessary to have witnesses for a baptism, as in the case of the Ethiopian eunuch, in **acts 8**. The only witness that he had was Philip who baptised him. But it makes for a good service to have a baptism in front of the whole church. The church can rejoice with the candidate. Even people that don't regularly go to church turn up. This includes unsaved relatives and friends of the one being baptised, who have come to watch. This is a good opportunity for the gospel can be preached to them.

I have heard of people baptising themselves in the bath. It does not mean any the less. It is the result of a Spiritual thing within them, leading them. The Holy Spirit will do His work within people, but we can hinder this work. It is hindered in many ways by the doctrines and traditions of men.

The second piece of symbolism is this. It is recognised that as we go down under the water, it is a symbol of the death of Jesus. As Christ died so are we dying to our self, Putting to death our old life, by going down under the water. Then as we come up, we are being raised up to a new life. The coming out of the water representing the resurrection of Jesus from the grave. The start of a new walk, a new life led by the Spirit. Walking in faith. Walking by the Spirit. It is also symbolism of being washed clean of our sin, as we go down into the water, being raised up clean and with a new pure and righteous spirit.

And I say walk by the Spirit, and you will not carry out the desire of the flesh. Galatians 5:16

A Way Of Thinking!

How many times have you been discussing something with other people, and some pipes up with the phrase," well to my way of thinking." When it comes to the work of the Holy Spirit; in bringing people to the point, where they realise the need to repent, and be born again. Then after this to the desire to be baptised; what has your way of thinking got to do with anything. Especially if it not Gods way of thinking. Again, as I have said before, and will continue to say; The Holy Spirit will do its work, teaching and leading. We should not hinder this We have no right to overrule God in this way.

The Holy Spirit can work in a small child, to cause them to want to follow Jesus. The Holy Spirit can cause them to want to be baptised. The Holy Spirit can come upon them just as well as it came, on the day of Pentecost. Then you say, "well to my way of thinking, this shouldn't happen." your way of thinking is wrong." We should be thinking Gods way of thinking. Trying to work all of this out intellectually takes us away from the walk of faith, our way of thinking is the world's way of thinking, not God's. Proverbs states a couple of times:

'There is a way that seems right to a man, but it's end is the way of death.' Proverbs16:25

Many people have walked away from faith in the Lord, simply because of 'Man's' way of thinking. Traditions and doctrines of men. I have spoken to a few people that say that they don't go to church, or have given up on Christianity, because of the hypocrisy within the church. Or they do not agree with some of the things that that church teaches or does. The mainstream, and also there a lot of charismatic churches, have adopted things that are not biblical. Maybe they have taken a hold of one or two biblical things and made an emphasis upon them. To the point that becomes a doctrine that is taken out of context with the truth.

See to it that no one takes you captive through philosophy and empty deception, according to the tradition of men, according to the elementary principles of the world, rather than according to Christ. Colossians2:8

I see the story of the rich young ruler who came to Jesus asking, "what shall I do to enter the Kingdom of God?" In the end Jesus told him to sell all his possessions and give to the poor. The rich man was sad at this. Then Jesus told His disciples, "that it is easier for a camel to go through the eye of a needle that a rich man to enter the kingdom of God." This astonished the disciples, they said, "then who can be saved?"

Jesus went on to tell His disciples that, "With men it impossible, but With God all things are possible." This is to do with man's way of thinking verses God's way of thinking. Jesus was not telling the rich man to become poor. He did not say give everything to the poor. The point of the story was to show that we should not rely on man's way of thinking, but to follow Christ, rather than to rely on the wealth. To put God first in all things.

Baptismal service

If I am thinking Gods way of thinking, I see that the baptismal service should probably be this way. A time of praise and worship, with thanksgiving. Then the preaching of the Gospel. This should then be followed with an alter call, or the baptism before the alter call. If there is anyone who responds the alter call and accepts Jesus as their Saviour, they should then be encouraged to be baptised there and then. They confess Jesus as Lord.; the water is there; The minister is wet already; there should be no hindrance. No matter whether it is Men, women, or children.

As far as I remember over the last forty years, I have only witnessed this happening once. Normally people are asked to come forward after the service has ended and talk to someone. If anybody responds, they may be led to Jesus at that time, but they are then encouraged to come to church. Take some time to find out what the Christian faith is all about, with the hope of planning a baptism at some future date. This is the wisdom of man, working against the wisdom of God, the work of the Holy Spirit at the point of salvation for that person has most probably been quenched.

This should not happen ever. To quench the Spirit in this way, is to put a stumbling block before the newborn Christian. Hindering the growth of their relationship with their Lord. It is especially bad if we relate it to children. If you preach the whole Gospel, you have to include baptism. If you have preached the whole gospel, and people believe and want to be baptised, you cannot then say, "Well we need to take you through a series of classes first, to prepare you for baptism." This is the tradition and doctrines of men!

'Repent(believe) and be baptised.

If we do not include the need for baptism in the preaching of the gospel, we are only preaching a part gospel. We need to be preaching the whole gospel. Believe and be baptised.

Why do we make it so difficult for a person to be baptised? Should we not be always be ready to baptise any person that receives Jesus as their Saviour, at that very point in time. I know that someone will say, "but we have to turn on the heating for the baptismal water. And it takes two hours to heat up. It is a waste of energy and money if we don't have to baptise anyone.

I say, "What has that got to do with anything." You may talk about saving energy because of global warming, save the planet! We know how this planet will end; it is written in the bible. It will be at the time that God has decided, not of mankind's doing. There is no excuse, every excuse you can think of is, ' to man's way of thinking,' not God's. What are you going to say the next time a child comes to you and says that 'I want to be baptised?' I would say, "Get you swimming kit, let's go to the pool and get it done.

Can I put it any stronger than this?
This brings me to a new point, a question. who can baptise a person? Does it have to be an ordained minister? Different people will have different views on this. I can understand why this is. The first thing is very obvious, whoever does the baptising must be a believer. The rule that the baptiser must be an ordained man, I think comes from the Jewish law, that children should be taken to the temple to be consecrated or presented to god by the priest. The child would be named. The priest as part of the consecration would circumcise the boys. And offer prayers up to God. This is clearly where the church took the idea of christening from.

That is the law that was given to the Israelites. The priests were originally people who were ordained by God. Many of the leaders at the head of our churches are men who have been through bible school/college and became ordained by man. Some have not even been born again, baptised and filled with the Holy Spirit.

Now here is a thought. Has not every born again, baptised, filled with the holy Spirit believer been ordained by God? You can argue this thought if you wish, but look what it says here in the first letter of Peter.

But you are a chosen race, a royal priesthood, a Holy nation, a people for God's own possession, that you may proclaim the excellencies of Him who has called you out of darkness into His marvelous light. 1 Peter 2:9

I do not think that baptism has to be done by an ordained man/person. Anyone who is a believer baptised and filled with the Spirit person is qualified to baptise. How great it would be for fathers to baptise their own children. It could be done under the direction of the leadership of the church. On the other hand, it does not need to be done during a church service at all. As I said you can go to the swimming pool and baptise. I have seen quite a few baptisms performed in the local swimming pool, with a small group of witnesses.

You know what children, and even some adults can be like. They will have the Holy Spirit put the idea into their hearts and say why can't I be baptised now? There is no reason why you cannot just fill the bath and baptise. It has been done before and will be done again. What you should not do is make excuses why a person cannot be baptised now.

I think that it is good to take a baby to church, and have them blessed and make a commitment to raise them up in the way of the Lord. I am not opposed to this. But to call the pouring of water upon a baby's head, baptism is not a biblical principle. It is a doctrine of man.

A parent can only take the responsibility of training a child in the things of God, they cannot take responsibility for the salvation of their child.

The child has to receive Jesus as Lord and then be baptised. There is only one way to the father, and that is through Jesus Christ. Doing things His way. Jesus was not baptised until He was thirty years old. It could not be done until John the Baptist was on the scene preparing the way for Jesus. Then Jesus told us what to do. Preach the good news, and baptise those who believe.

Chapter 5: Spiritual Gifts The Tools We Need

<u>The Mind Of Christ</u>

For who among men knows the thoughts of a man, except the spirit of the man which is in him? Even so the thoughts of God no one knows except the Spirit of God. Now we have received, not the spirit of the world, but the Spirit that is from God, so that we that we may know the things freely given to us by God. 1 Corinthians 2:11-12

These verses say, that we have received the Spirit form God. The Holy Spirit, so that we may know what God has freely given. Let's put it another way, If we are not born again, we cannot receive the Holy Spirit, and we cannot know the things that God has freely given. The Holy Spirit cannot reside within a person that has not been born again.

God and sin cannot reside together. Do you wish for your children to know what God has freely given to them? Part of the work of the Holy Spirit, in the process of being born again, is to reveal to us the mind of Christ. This is even more so once baptized in the Holy Spirit and speaking in tongues.

Paul says in Corinthians that When speaking in tongues we are speaking the mysteries of God, that means, that God can reveal things to us through speaking in tongues. The Spirit can and will reveal to us the mind of God. When are speaking the language of God. It is the Holy Spirit talking through us in direct communication to God, what the Spirit hears He will tell us.

The Holy Spirit is an essential part of the life of a Christian. It is through the Holy Spirit that we can come to know what God's will for us is, and our lives. Without the guidance of the Holy Spirit, we are just walking aimlessly in the dark. I believe and know that God talks to me. He is talking to me right now as I write. Guiding my thoughts and the words that I type. This is the work of the Holy Spirit. Just imagine the positive impact it would have upon your family life to have your children hearing direct from God! Let alone the life of your church. As Jesus said,

"He will glorify Me, for He will take of mine and disclose it to you. All things that the Father has are Mine; therefore I said that He takes of Mine and will disclose it to you." John 16;15-16

God's word says that we have the mind of Christ, that in and through our Spirit we know all things, but all things are not revealed to us at the same time, we know things as we need them. God knows all things and would not give us more knowledge than we can handle. That is where spiritual growth comes in. God allows us to know, what we can manage. As we become stronger in the faith, he shows us more and more, as we are able to understand it. If that is the way He works with us as adults, He knows just how much knowledge a child can manage.

Again How and why are pointless questions. God is able to use children so much more than we can imagine. Just as He would love to use us as adults more than we are able to understand. If only we would allow Him to. This is true Just as much with children. The Holy Spirit can give a child wisdom beyond the understanding of their years. We can all access the mind of Christ through our spirits, which is in communion with the Holy Spirit.

For who has known the mind of the Lord, that he will instruct Him? But we have the mind of Christ. 1 Corinthians 2:16

We understand that Jesus was God the Son come in the flesh. Yes this is right, but He was a man just as we are. He had the limitations of a man. He had to rely on the Holy Spirit to do the works that He did. He understood and was able to harness the power of the Holy Spirit. He did this to teach to us how to use and harness the power of the Holy Spirit. When He was on the earth, Jesus did not know all things; He said so, talking about when He comes back:

"But of that day and hour no one knows, not even the angels, nor the Son, but the Father alone." Matthew 24:36

There are other places in the new testament too, that show that Jesus did not know all things. The woman with the issue of blood touched the hem of His garment and was healed, and He turned around asking "who touched me." Jesus knew that healing had flown out of Him, but He did not know who it was who touched Him, or what the healing was. The disciples said to Him that there were many people pressing around Him, of course someone touched you! until the woman told Him. He did not know who it was.

Jesus operated in the gifts of the Holy Spirit, just as we have to. He used words of knowledge, to call Philip. Also, to call Zacchaeus to down from the Sycamore tree. Then too there was the Samaritan woman at the well. His preaching was, very much words of wisdom. He operated in faith and used the gift of healing wherever He went. He performed miracles and prophesied.

The only gifts of the Holy Spirit that it seems that Jesus did not use were the gifts tongues. He may have done this during His times of private prayer. Though He did speak to non-Jewish people, who maybe did not speak Hebrew. It is a good possibility that he was able to speak any language through the power of the Holy Spirit. After all God does understand every language on the earth.

Jesus The Man

The fact is that Jesus was a man, who operated as a man filled and anointed with the Holy Spirit. Using the gifts of the Spirit. He did not begin His ministry until He had received the Holy Spirit. He did not do any miracles, no healings, until after He had resisted the temptations of the devil, at the end of a forty day fast. Up until then and through His ministry, He had lived a life of faith just as Abraham had.

Jesus was born as a Human baby. He had to grow and learn just as every other child that was around Him, learn to talk, to eat without covering His face with His food. He had to learn to walk just the same as everyone. He learned to read, which was probably something He excelled at more than most. He had to learn to control His bowels and bladder like all of us. He sweated and smelled just as bad as everyone around Him, so He had to wash. He was a child who grew into a man. He had to learn.

He had to grow. He had to go through the same processes as we all do. He could have chosen to concentrate on just the carpentry skills taught by His father, but He chose His heavenly Fathers path. He chose to walk in the Lord God.

Jesus was presented to the Lord, at the temple in Jerusalem, as was the custom to offer sacrifices and dedicate Him to the Lord. Part of this was the covenant God made with Abraham, the act of circumcision. After this, it says that they returned to Nazareth,

And the child continued to grow and become strong, increasing in wisdom; and the grace of God. Luke 2:40

Later when He was twelve, and His parents took Him to the Passover feast, it says that He sneaked off and His parents did not know that He was not with them in the caravan of people, on the way home. Not until a day had passed, did they start looking for Jesus and could not find Him.

They returned to Jerusalem to look for Him and found Him in the temple after three days. He was amazing the teachers at His understanding, and answers to their questions. When they got back home it says, that Jesus continued in subjection to his parents.

And Jesus kept increasing in wisdom and stature, and in favor with God and men. Luke 2:52

It was a process of learning. Jesus did not just know everything because He was the Son of God. He had to grow in the wisdom of God. He had to become strong in the knowledge of God, He had to learn. Jesus had to develop into the man of God He became. Some who read this might cry out in disbelief or anger at what I have just said but look at the verse above from Luke 2:52. Jesus *increased* in wisdom. Jesus *increased* in stature. Jesus *increased* in favor. With God and men. Look at it again, it was a process that He went through. A process of learning. He did not yet have the Holy

Spirit to teach and guide Him. He was a man, the second Adam, as it says,

So also it is written, "The first man, Adam, Became a living soul." The last Adam (Jesus) became a life-giving Spirit. 1 Corinthians15:45

Jesus became a Life-giving Spirit. This was when He was transfigured and ascended into heaven. On earth He had an earthly body born into sin, but He did not sin, even if He had it would have been forgiven through His death. All the sin of the world was put on Jesus at the Cross.

That is why God turned His face from Him, and Jesus said, "My God, My God, why have you forsaken me." Through the one-man sin entered the world, So, through the man Jesus, God made a way for all to come and be in His presence. He became a life-giving Spirit. The Spirit of the Living God, the resurrected Jesus. is alive in us.

In Jesus we live and move and have our being Acts 17:28 NABRE

Role Of The Holy Spirit

This is important to everything that I am saying in this book. We have to understand what it is, that The Spirit of God does. What His function is. What is the reason that God sends the Spirit into us. Then understand that if the Spirit is able to do those things in us, then He is able and willing to do the same for our children. I believe that our children need the use of the work of the Spirit in their lives, maybe even more than we do.

This is a perception, in the fact that we have learned and come to rely upon our own abilities. So, by default we tend not to rely upon the guidance of the Spirit so much. If a child can learn to rely upon the Spirit from an early age, then He is more likely to do so when he gets older, having witnessed the results of reliance on the Spirit. Why would they want to live any other way?

The gift is for you and your children

God's gift to us as born-again Christians is the Holy Spirit. It is to help us. Jesus called Him the Helper, the comforter, the teacher, and the Guide. His role is to do all these things and more. Here are some of the things that Jesus said the Holy Spirit will do. Convict the world concerning sin, righteousness, and judgment. If you are born again, you were already convicted of these, that's how you came to know that you needed to be born again.

The Holy Spirit did this for us. This is talking about convicting the world, the people that do not believe, so that they may see the truth and become born again. Once we are born again, it is our own heart, our conscience, that might condemn us, convict us, when we do not do something right. We become guilty in our selves. It is not the Spirit making us feel bad, that is not what the Spirit does. It is our own conscience, our own heart.

We are of the truth, and will assure our heart and quiet our conscience before Him, whenever our heart convicts us [in guilt]; for God is greater that our heart, and He knows all things [nothing is hidden from Him because we are in His hands] 1 John 3:19-20 AMP

The Holy Spirit the helper, the enabler, the strengthener, the equipper. This is not an exhaustive list, but it shows what is meant by the helper. You become enabled, strengthened, equipped to do somethings that are too difficult for you in your own strength. I know that many of us as adults would benefit from this help.

How much more would children benefit? Trouble is, that for too many hundreds of years we have denied that children can be led by the Spirit. Even that the help of the Holy Spirit is even available at all, by way of the use of the gifts of the Spirit. Instead children have to be led, guided only by parents.

We allow them to be guided by teachers, friends, the TV, or internet. None of which are of any great benefit, in the real scheme of things as far as God is concerned. Parents should be guiding children to become more reliant on the leading of the Spirit. The Holy Spirit helping your children has to be, is the greatest help they will ever get. Because the help comes from God.

The holy Spirit will teach us all things, and bring to our remembrance things that Jesus said, Not only that, Jesus said the Spirit will guide us into all truth, What He hears (from the Father) He will tell us. He will also tell us of things to come. Another aspect that Jesus said about the Holy Spirit is this. That when we have to speak out, because we have been challenged by someone, or some authority for our faith, we should not worry about how we should answer, or speak, because the Spirit will give us the words we need when we need them.

Jesus also said to His disciples, that they will have more benefit from having the Holy Spirit, than having His physical person with them. The reason for this is that while they had Jesus walking, talking, teaching, the only power they had was, that which was delegated to them from Jesus.

They did not have the power of the Holy spirit flowing through them. When Jesus died the power departed from the disciples. When Jesus left the Spirit left with Him. This is why later on after His resurrection, Jesus told them to wait until the Holy Spirit comes. This is when the fulfillment, of the role of the Holy Spirit, will begin.

Baptism In The Holy Spirit

Here we go, something that a lot of adults within the Christian world cannot agree upon for themselves, let alone even contemplating the thought of children being baptised in the Holy Spirit. Many think that this is something that no longer happens. They don't believe that the gifts of the Spirit are in use today, or even relevant. Some believe that they died out with the apostles.

They say that only the occasional person anointed by God are able to utilize the Spiritual gifts. People like those who have been canonized and made saints. Some even say that those who operate in the gifts of the Spirit, are not using the Spirit of God but, the power is demonic. This is actually a lie, perpetuated by the devil.

You have to read and understand what the word of God really says about the baptism in the Holy Spirit. In the book of Acts, (The acts of the Holy Spirit), it was not just the 120 that were gathered in the upper room that were baptised in the Spirit. There are many more instances where people received this gift from God. Which empowered them to go spread the good news, performing miracles, healings, even just to be able to just get up and speak with boldness, as Peter did.

It has been said that the Church is in decline, I have been hearing this for many years in the United Kingdom. And it may well be, within the mainstream church denominations. Could this have something to do with the rejection of the teaching about the Holy Spirit and it's gifts? It is certainly an aspect and something to think about. The fact is that the fastest growing churches are usually ones that operate in the gifts of the Spirit.

I declare that we need the baptism of the Holy Spirit. We cannot function as believers in the way that God planned without it. We need Him to comfort, teach, help and guide us; through this life, now more than ever before in the history of the Church. Without it we are just being religious. That is doing things without the power and anointing of the Spirit of the Living God.

Jesus said that, "In my name you will lay hands on the sick and they shall recover, you will cast out demons, you will raise the dead." When was the last time that you raised someone from the dead? I am talking to myself here too.

Think of this, if every born -again spirit filled Christian raised someone from the dead, there would be a revival like the world has never seen before. Even if every born-again Spirit filled Christian laid hands on someone sick and they recovered, it would bring an impressive revival.

These signs will accompany those who believed: in My Name they shall cast out demons, they will speak with new tongues; they will pick up serpents, and if they drink any deadly poison, it will not hurt

them; they will lay hands on the sick and they will recover. Mark 16:17-18

It is not God that will bring revival, it is Spirit filled children of God. People who are allowing the gifts of the Spirit to flow through them. God works through His people, through the Holy Spirit. He always has worked through people. He always will work through people. He will work through anybody who will allow the Holy Spirit to lead them.

Adults and children. Children need to be taught that they need the baptism in the Holy Spirit. For the most, in our churches this is not even taught to the adults, let alone children. I cannot ever remember hearing this teaching in church, unless I went to some special event, with a visiting preacher.

'For the gift is for you and your children.'

We pray many times expecting God to do things, that He has told us to do. Things like asking God to heals us, or to heal someone else. When God says, "You will lay hands on the sick and they will recover." Some spiritual people may pray for God to make the devil leave them alone, when God says, "You resist the devil and he will flee from you."

It is an act, an act of faith. The power of God is not out there somewhere with God, to use as He pleases. He has placed that power inside of us, through the baptism in the Holy Spirit. This is the power that God has given to us to use, to live a victorious, abundant life.

The Power of the Holy Spirit that is inside of us, if we are baptised in the Holy Spirit, is the same power that God used when He created the world and all that is within it. It is the same power that was flowing through

Jesus during His three years of Ministry. It is the same power that raised Jesus from the dead. It is the same power that flowed through the apostles, and many others in the early church. It is inside us. We just have to use it. It is activated by using it. Faith is the key to activating the power of the Holy Spirit.

God does not do anything except through people. It has always been that way. Read all the stories in the bible, God uses people. He always will use people to make His will come to pass. That is why He had to send His Son in the human body of Jesus. He had to use a person, Jesus, to take away the sin of the world. Are you a human, and have the Holy Spirit? Then you are a good candidate for God to use.

The bible tells us that the sacrifices of animals would not, could not fulfill the requirement of the law. That is why it had to be repeated over and over. The Bible also say that Jesus came and died ONCE, for all. For all sin, for all people, for all time.

For the death that He died, He died to sin once for all; but He life that He lives he live to god. Romans 6:10

In Hebrews it talks about priests having to sacrifice again and again for the sins of people, but Jesus died once for all, this is so that, No sacrifice ever had to be made again, for all time! God used a man as a sacrifice to bring us into relationship with Him. God also allowed the devil to use men to bring about His will for the sacrifice of Jesus.

The bible says that when Jesus ascended, he sat down and gave gifts to men (mankind), these are the nine Spiritual gifts, and the seven ministerial gifts. They all come with the baptism of the holy Spirit. The Holy

Spirit is a gift, from God to empower us to live victorious, abundant lives. We cannot be the people that God wants us to be without the Holy Spirit.

<u>Can children be baptised in the Holy Spirit?</u>

And it shall be in the last days; God says, that I shall pour out My Spirit on all mankind Acts 2:17

There is absolutely no reason why not. In the beginning of God pouring His Holy spirit on the day of Pentecost, Peter stood up and declared some amazing things. 'I will pour out My spirit on all flesh', is the way that the King James version puts it. All means all. Not just those who are old enough. Or mature enough, or clever enough. It is not like going to an amusement park, where you have to be a certain age, or height in order to ride on certain rides. There is no age limit on the baptism of the Holy Spirit. Peter also said this at the time,

"The gift is for you and your children." Acts 2:39

Peter had just been filled with the Holy Spirit and speaking in tongues. Maybe this was an interpretation, we don't know. He was speaking as a fulfillment of a prophesy of Jesus. Jesus said that, "When you are called to give account for your faith, do not worry about what you should say, as the Holy spirit will give you the words, at that time. So, speaking under the leading of the Holy Spirit, Peter said.

"The gift is for you and your children."

These are the words of God spoken through Peter. If the gift of the Holy Spirit was not for our children too, then he would not have specifically said children. I think that if God were to categorize people, there would be four groups. Men, Women, Children, and unbelievers. God does not want that anyone should be an unbeliever. In this instance, Peter was speaking to unbelievers, so that leaves men, women, and children.

Let's look at some examples in the bible, of children of all ages that were used by God. We will start with Samuel. He was dedicated to the Lord by his mother, before he was even conceived. Given to the High Priest as a baby. He was raised under the instruction of the High Priest into the ways of God.

Samuel became a prophet as a young boy. He heard Gods voice calling his name. Samuel thought it was the priest calling him, and so woke him up. After the Third time of being woken up, the priest realised that it had been God that was calling Samuel and instructed him on what to do if God called him again. Samuel received his first prophesy, it was about the High priest, and his family.

There was also the dreamer, Joseph. He was having some amazing dreams. I would like to think that he had dreams all through his childhood. Then as a teenager, about seventeen years old, the dreams seam to take on a greater significance. Understanding that his brothers were somewhat jealous of Joseph, because of his favor with their father Jacob.

For them to hear these dreams would sound like Joseph was getting a bit full of himself. So, his dreams about his brothers bowing down to him was a dream too far. Too much for them to accept. So much so that, if it were not for the wisdom of the oldest brother Reuben, Joseph would have been killed.

What about Sampson, he was dedicated to the lord before conception. Not just by His parents, But God called Him to be a type of Savior for the Israelites, before he was born. You need to understand this: he did not get his great strength as an adult. It was not just fleeting, now and again things that came upon him from time to time.

His great strength came though his commitment to god. (There is a great message right in that statement, a commitment to the Lord will make you strong). He did not have to go to the gym three or more times a week to build himself up. Sampson's strength grew as he grew. He was always so much the strongest, fastest, Child in his town and country. You know he never got bullied! Who would dare? It was not his hair that made him strong, his hair was a sign of his commitment. It had never been cut, since his birth. Committed and called by god since way before his birth.

How about Jeremiah? Called as a prophet, as a young man, maybe a teenager. And how he complained to god that he was too young to speak out the word of God, because of his youth. Afraid of what people might think of him as he was so young. Look at what God had said to Jeremiah:

"Before I formed you in the womb, I knew you. And before you were born, I Consecrated you; I have appointed you a prophet to the nations."
Jeremiah 1:4

Amazing that God can know you before you are even a twinkle in your father's eye. Not only that God can call you and have a work for you to do. You may not believe this is true, but it says that He knew Jeremiah before he was conceived. David said something similar about himself in: **Psalm 139:15-16**

Then there was Timothy, a young man who had grown up in the wisdom and the knowledge of the Lord. Under the direction, teaching and influence of his mother. Who must have been a women greatly used by God, because Paul says of Timothy, "The Spirit that was in your mother is in you. That is the holy Spirit, that used him mightily working alongside Paul.

There are more, surely many more that the bible does not tell you about. I will tell you of one more. John the Baptist was filled with the Holy Spirit in his mother's womb. It says that the baby John leapt inside the womb. This as when he heard the sound of Mary's voice. The anointing was so great that John's mother Elisabeth began to prophesy over Mary and her son Jesus yet to be born.

When you study scripture and see all of the marvelous things that the Holy Spirit has done; it can be hard to believe this truth. That all of that mighty power, is at work in us as born-again Spirit filled believers. Trying to understand this truth is impossible to us, even to be able to cope with this knowledge.

How could we expect a child to understand and cope with this awesome power? It is the wrong question, the right question might be; What are the characteristics of children that I should seek to emulate, in order to be more open to the leading of the Holy Spirit?

We tend to think that all power and authority is with God. Let me put it another way; we have been programmed to think that it is up to God to direct His power to where He needs it when He needs it. That everything, every aspect of the use of His power is down to God. That all we have to do is convince God to act on our behalf. This is not what the word of God says.

God has put that power, and authority, within every born-again Holy Spirit filled believer. It is in us. We are the conduits of Gods power through the Holy Spirit. We just need to know and learn how to let the power flow. As I said before, God uses men to work through. That is the way He has chosen to do things.

Sometimes He will use angels to protect us, in some sudden, unpredictable circumstances.

It is like this. You have electricity flowing to your house. You have the authority to use that power. You just have to plug in your appliance and switch on the switches. If you don't flick the switch, you can't use the power. The power is there, but it is not being utilised until you switch the switch. You don't call the power company to turn the electric on every time you need to use it. You have already the authority to use the power. It is the same with many Spirit filled Christians, the power is there, but it is not being utilised.

If we as adults don't know how to utilise the power of the Holy Spirit, we cannot see or understand how children can utilise the power. If this is the truth with adult Spirit filled Christians. How are we to expect or think that it would, should work, or be available to children? Here is a thought, a way of thinking that seems to be normal.

If WE are not using/utilising the power of the Holy Spirit, how can we even begin to think that children can use that power? We have the power of the Holy Spirit, but we do not use it much, if ever. We should be relying on that power everyday of our lives. To help us make the right decisions, do the right things, say the right words.

Too much we rely on our own understanding. Our own intellect, our own way of thinking. We ought to spend more time listening for the leading of the Spirit As adults we have many doubts about the power of the Holy Spirit. A lot of people doubt that it exists for our use anymore. That this gift of God ceased to be after the early apostles died. That this life transforming power died with those apostles. We doubt that it would, or that it is working for us. Will it, can it work through us?

This doubt can come because of having spent too many years being influenced by the spirit that is in the world. The holy Spirit is in us, not of the world but from God. The spirit of the world is a spirit of unbelief and produces doubt as a fruit. This even has come in some ways, through the things that we have been taught in church. This really, is a sad fact of life. If you can be born again so can children. If you can be baptised in the Holy Spirit, So can children. If you can flow in the power, so can children.

Another thought is this; we see and the power of the holy Spirit flowing out through other people. Men and women, we see as gifted of god. We do not even begin to think that God would use us in this way. We have the same Spirit. It is true, that people that are operating in the use of the Gifts of the spirit, can actually operate in all the gifts. Certainly not all at the same time. The Holy spirit will normally, flow through different people, in different gifts. As it says in 1 Corinthians 12:4-11

But one and the same Spirit works all these things, distributing to each one individually just as He wills. 1 Corinthians 12:11

For the gift is for you and your children.

I have seen children as young as seven years old, operating in some of the gifts of the Spirit; Speaking in tongues; receiving words of knowledge; words of wisdom, Prophesying, healings. Think of this, if you teach a child that if they lay hands on the sick, the sick will be healed. They will believe it. They will do it and expect the healing to take place.

That is how faith works. If you teach a child to ask God for Knowledge, or wisdom in any situation, when they have a problem they will pray, and expect God to answer. The gifts of faith, healing, knowledge and wisdom usually work together. They work together with faith, if your unbelief is greater than your faith then your unbelief will rule.

We have been taught that if we feel ill, we have to go to the doctor, We pass this way of thinking on to our children. On the other hand, if we started walking by faith, and instead of running to the doctor first. If we sought after God, and the power of His Spirit to flow through us. We could do much to lift the burdens of the health services. If we as adults got into the position of relying on God more for ALL of our needs, then our children would learn that this is the right way and would seek Gods solutions to their problems.

It is not just doctors and illness, it about every area of our lives. Health, wealth, work, relationships. If we are baptised in the Holy Spirit, the Holy Spirit is within us ready to help in anything we need. It has gifts from the Father for us to utilise. Gifts that will enable us to live victorious, abundant lives. Why would anyone not want this? Why would you not want it for your children?

The bible says that the gifts of the Holy Spirit are for the building up of the church. This you will know and understand. In the same way the gifts are for use in everyday life. For your personal use to build you up in the wisdom and knowledge of the Lord. We need to get this thought and idea into our hearts and minds. Because when you use these gifts of the Spirit in everyday life situations, you are more able to help the people in the church to be built up. If you allow yourself to be built up, you are then in a position Spiritually to be able to help others Spiritually.

The gifts of the Spirit are, wisdom, knowledge, faith, gifts of healings, miracles, prophesy, distinguishing of spirits, various types of tongues, and interpreting of tongues. These are all of great benefit to us in our daily lives. Distinguishing of spirits and words of knowledge, and wisdom will greatly help us to deal with the different people that we meet each day. Also to help protect us from anything, from the spirit that is in the world, that may come against us through other people, or situations.

The Spirit of God is teaching me here as I write this, as I have not really thought much in the past about the gifts being used in this way. I knew it to be true but not really applied it in this way too much until recently.

I was studying walking by faith and not by sight, **1 Corinthians 5:7,** connected to walking by the Spirit, and not carrying out the desires of the flesh, **Galatians 5:16-18** Seeing again in a more detail that walking by the Spirit requires faith. You cannot walk by the Spirit, without walking by faith. Walking by faith is to live the whole of our lives by faith.

By connection walking by the Spirit involves the whole of our lives. Therefore, if you are baptised in the Spirit, walking in the Spirit with use of the Spiritual gifts, they will become evident in use in daily lives. Why would you not use the free gifts of God to help you daily, not just in crisis situations. The power is within you to use for God's glory. Every day! In your lives as well as your children's.

Chapter 6: Children And The Use Of Spiritual Gifts

What if our children received the baptism in the Holy Spirit, and began operating in the gifts of the Holy Spirit? How awesome would that be. Building each other up in the Lord. You are helping your children, and your children helping you. Having a mutual respect for the various gifts that the whole family has.

It would be like a mini church, all bringing something to build up the family together. To a child a gift of knowledge, to a parent the gift of wisdom. To another child the gift of tongues, to the other parent the gift of interpretation. I believe that a family can work this way.

This is the way that God wants His church to work. He does not work it so that there is one person that is the only person to use the gifts of the Spirit. In the same way He does not want that just the head of the family has all the control of Spiritual things. Yes, the head is the head, and he has the decision-making authority. But he needs to listen to what the Spirit is saying though the other members of the family.

I think that normally parents do not take the time to listen to what their children have to say about some things, simply because they think that whatever they are dealing with is an adult's problem. Yet God is able and does give wisdom to a child. He will use children to speak His word.

So, let's take a look at the Spiritual gifts and their applications. Look at how they benefit us as adults, in the church, and how they may be utilised by children. It is easy for adults to have a haughty attitude towards children, because adults have had many more years of gaining knowledge and have learned how to use that knowledge.

It must be understood first, by everyone, that not all knowledge is good. I know that, in part it depends upon how you use the knowledge. There is some truth in the fact that much of what we learn is a corruption of the truth. What I mean is that the worlds way of thinking is not necessarily the God's way of thinking.

The various gifts of tongues. This is not the first in the list, as it is in the bible, but it I want to start here. For this reason, it is probably the one gift of all that is the most controversial of the gifts. But there are four variations to the gift of tongues. For this reason I think it is important, for out of the gift of tongues can also come words of wisdom, knowledge and prophesy.

1 Tongues as a sign to unbelievers.

So Then tongues are a sign, not to those who believe but to unbelievers. 1 Corinthians 14:22

This is what happened on the day of Pentecost. Believers were gathered together in the upper room, when the Holy Spirit came upon them, and they began to speak in other tongues. They were speaking languages that could not be understood by them, yet they were speaking recognised languages. Not recognisable to themselves. Languages that were recognisable the people from other countries who were there. People that did not speak the local Hebrew language.

People from various countries, heard the disciples speaking in their own language, different disciples speaking different languages. Unbelievers who would not have understood a word of Hebrew, turning to God because they could understand what was being said. The Holy Spirit gave the believers the ability to speak a foreign language for the benefit of unbelievers.

We have become a multicultural society, not just in the UK, but within a lot of countries now. I go to work at the swimming pool that I work, sometimes I end up speaking in tongues quietly as I get changed into or out of my work uniform. As I hear other people talking in the cubicles around, so many are speaking a foreign language to me.

Sometimes have the thought, what would happen if I started speaking in tongues as loud as some of these other people are speaking, would anybody be able to understand what I am saying? Of course, it would have to be as the Spirit led me, and it might happen as the thought is there in my mind. I am sure that the Lord could use that to reach somebody.

Our children as well as us live in this multicultural society. And it could be possible for them and us to speak in tongues of another language, of someone around them and speak the word of God into that person's life, or multiple people. I know that this can be done, if that is what God wills. He did it on the day of Pentecost.

What a great blessing it would be. I am sure that this happened many times in the early church. Although it does not actually mention this, the word of god spread across the world at such a great rate, to many nations of different languages. I have read of and spoken to people who were preaching, without an interpreter, to people of different language and the people understood what was being said.

2 For edification of the church/for interpretation.

A sign to believers. This is two of the variations here, the gift of tongues for the Church and the interpretation. This is where someone stands up in a church gathering and begins to speak out in tongues, as led by the Holy Spirit. There needs to be an interpretation, so that the whole church can be edified, built up, by what has been said.

The interpretation could be a word of prophesy, knowledge, or wisdom. What if this began to happen within our families too? The wealth of blessings that would begin to flow from God to and through each member of the family would be great. In the family is where we can begin to encourage children to use the gift of tongues. It should become a natural everyday thing to do. Both for children and for the parents

I have heard of this, happening around the world in various places. That a preacher or teacher has gone, spoke tongues on television. And someone watching has understood what was said, even though the person who spoke in tongues did not realise it was a known language.

Also situations where the preacher for one reason or another has not got an interpreter, has gone on to preach anyway, and the whole congregation have heard their own language, even though the preacher as far as he is concerned has preached in, his own language. One case where the preacher spoke in English, and one or more persons heard the message preached in Spanish.

We cannot underestimate the power that comes through the speaking in tongues, the wisdom and knowledge that will flow to us, and through us. If we speak in tongues it is the Spirit of God speaking through us. If we get an interpretation, it is God speaking to us. So, you had better take notice, even if it comes through a child. The speaking in tongues within a group of believers can be misused though. This is spoken of much by Paul, to the church of the Corinthians. Regarding the misuse of the gift.

Therefore if the whole church gathers together and all speak in tongues, and ungifted men or unbelievers enter, will they not say that you are mad? 1 Corinthians 14:23

Paul Is trying to teach that everything should be done in an orderly fashion, not in confusion. That the spoken word is better done so everyone can understand, than that nobody understands what is being said. That the church, and any unbelievers that might be with them can be built up in faith.

Too many people speaking out in tongues at once is not good for the unbelievers. They will think that it is just too much confusion and not want to come back. Unbelievers do not understand this gift, and will not unless it is used in an orderly manner within the church. Even many Christians do not understand this gift. A sad fact, as it is a big thing in the life of especially Paul. The use of this gift can be taught to children too.

3 For self-edification.

This is probably the use of tongues that is not so easily understood, and so not regularly used by a lot of spirit filled Christians. Yet Paul clearly states that if you speak in tongues, you edify yourself. That is building yourself up, strengthening your faith. If you want to settle for a mediocre Christian life without the power of the Holy Spirit, you will not be a person that spends time personally speaking in tongues.

Why was Paul such a powerful force for the Lord. He says that He spoke in tongues more than all of the people in the Corinthian church. Not in the church, but in his private prayer life.

The one who speaks in a tongue edifies himself; but the one who prophesies Edifies the church.
1 Corinthians 14:4

They had controversy about speaking in tongues way back in the Corinthian Church, and Paul was writing to help them sort it out. Paul even says," I thank God that I speak in tongues more that all of you put together, but I would rather speak in church with words that everyone can understand. There is a place for speaking in tongues. Usually in your private prayer time, and even in church, but it should be done in a quiet manner. Not letting it dominate over the proceedings of the church meeting, unless there is an interpretation.

If we taught our children the importance of speaking in tongues for their own personal edification. It would be of great benefit to them. Not only that, but to the whole family. What a tremendous blessing it would be to have your children being led by the Spirit of the living God, instead of the spirits and principalities of this world. We all need this, adults and children.

But you, beloved, building yourselves up on your most holy faith, praying in the Spirit. Jude 1:20

Every born again, spirit filled believer in the Lord Jesus, has the ability to speak in tongues. By using this gift they build up their faith. Faith is a gift, you got it when you were born again. It is the faith of Jesus. It is not a question of little faith or big faith. We have been given the measure of faith. This is the same faith that Jesus had and used during His ministry on the earth.

We all have the same faith, but it can be counteracted by the amount of unbelief that we also have. This is a big problem within the Christian world. Too much unbelief over the gift of speaking or praying in tongues. Jesus said that we will speak in other tongues. It is a gift, that comes through the Holy Spirit. That goes along with all the other gifts. Before his death, he told His disciples before He died:

"Truly, truly, I say to you, He who believes in me, the works that I do, he will also, and greater works than these he will do, because I go to the Father." John 14:12

Later Jesus explains that, unless He goes back to the Father He cannot send the Holy Spirit. That the benefit of the Holy Spirit will be greater than having Jesus with them. The fact is that Jesus was a human being; a man just like you and me, but without the baggage of sin. This meant that Jesus could only be in one place at a time.

Touch and heal one or two people at a time. When He left the disciples to go and pray they were without Him. For instance, the episode in the boat when the storm came, then Jesus came along walking on the water. They were afraid thinking that they were going to die.

On the other hand When the Holy Spirit came, He was within each one of them and went with them wherever they went. The power of the Holy Spirit was directly flowing to them and through them. Just as it did through Jesus. This is true for us too. The Holy Spirit can be everywhere at the same time. Working, helping, teaching, using people all over the world at the same time, Healing, and all the other gifts of the Spirit; through everyone who believes. The power of the Holy Spirit should be flowing through us.

And these signs will accompany those who have believed: in My name they will cast out demons, they will speak with new tongues. Mark 26:17

The gift is for you and your children

You will notice a couple of things in the verse above the use of the word WILL. It does not say might or could if they want to. It says that they WILL! Cast out demons and Will Speak with new tongues. The second thing that I pick up from this verse is that it says, 'Those who have believed.' There is no age limit. Just those who have believed. There are no conditions either. Except they be filled with the Holy Spirit. Jesus said:

But you will receive power when the Holy Spirit comes upon you; ……. Acts 1:8

So maybe Jesus was expecting every born-again believer to be filled with all the fullness of the Holy Spirit. Why not? It is a gift of God. Jesus personally sent the Holy Spirit to us. Maybe man's will, has got in the way of accepting this gift. From personal experience I know that the gift of speaking in tongues, can seem difficult to accept. The holy Spirit is a gift from God to His children. You can choose to accept it, or not.

I spent a couple of years doubting that the gift of tongues that I was using was real. Thinking that I might be making it up by myself. I think that this can be a common problem. Again it is a question of faith verses unbelief.

Part of My problem was, I only personally knew of one other person that spoke in tongues at the time, and their speaking in tongues sounded different to mine. Even though I had been in meeting where plenty of people were speaking in tongues, and they all sounded different. I had a doubt in my mind. This was the devil, telling me it was not real, and planting doubt in my mind.

For if I pray in a tongue, my spirit prays, but my mind is unfruitful. 1 Corinthians 14:14

4 Words of wisdom

So let's go back to the list of the gifts of the Spirit. Continuing with the first in the list. The word of wisdom. Wisdom in this sense, is not the same as being wise. Knowing how the world works or having knowledge gained from many years of living and using your wisdom to your advantage.

I am talking about a supernatural wisdom that comes supernaturally, through the working of the Holy Spirit. Wisdom that is given to a person at any given point, to enable them to understand what to do in that particular situation. It is usually something you would not have naturally thought. A direction to do something or say something that maybe seems strange to you.

It is not always this way, it could be something that makes sense as plain as day, but you could not see it with your own mind. It is like the light switched on inside your mind. A sudden inspiration of the direction that you should go.

Words of wisdom very often come or go together with words of knowledge. For instance, you are thinking and praying about how to deal with a situation, or person. You get an understanding of what has caused the situation, (word of knowledge), then you get to know how to deal with the situation, (word of wisdom). You may, be praying for someone who needs healing, and you supernaturally get a word of knowledge, telling you that this is the reason for the sickness. Then you received a word of wisdom to show you how to deal with the cause.

I think that we can get words of wisdom at any time, about anything that happens in our lives. The Holy Spirit is given to help us in our walk with the Lord. There are many things in our personal world that try to hinder our walk. This true for all of us, whether it be a direct attack of the devil, or just the worlds way of thinking, or doing things.

Jesus said that we are in the world, but not of the world. This means that we can be affected, or even infected by the world. The worlds way of thinking and doing things. James tells us, about the tongue, how we are to use our words the wrong way or the right way. People speak out the wisdom of the world, and it sounds good and right to our mind, but James says this:

This wisdom is not that which comes down from above, but is earthly, natural, demonic. For where jealousy and selfish ambition exist, there is disorder, and every evil thing. But the wisdom that comes from above is first pure, then peaceable, gentle, reasonable, full of mercy and good fruits, unwavering, without hypocrisy. James 3:15-17

The wisdom of the world comes at us from every angle. We send our children into the world to go to school to be taught the wisdom of the world. Why would you not wish for them to have the Holy Spirit with them to give them God's wisdom, God's view on all that they see and hear. We need it as adults and our children need this too.

Yet we go about our daily lives without relying upon the wisdom of God, and expect our children to cope in the same way. This because we were never taught these things so we naturally think that our children will be OK, because, "We turned out OK!". We were taught to rely on the wisdom of the world, which is, 'earthly, natural, and demonic!' I like the book of 1 John, because it talks directly to people of different ages. See here what it says:

I have written to you little children, because your sins are forgiven for His names sake. I have written to you children because you know the Father. Do not love the world, nor the things in the world. If anyone loves the world, the love of the Father is not in him. 1 John 2:12, 13, 15

We need the wisdom of God in all areas of our lives. We all need it men, women and children. Any wisdom that comes through the holy Spirit will line up with the word of God. Without it we are like the blind leading the blind. We cannot rely upon the worlds systems to teach our children the right things. We need the wisdom that comes through the Holy Spirit, and so do our children.

5 Words of knowledge

As I mentioned before words of knowledge often accompany Words of wisdom. Also prophesy can come into both of these gifts of the Spirit. They will never ever contradict the word of God. They can also be words direct from the word of God, depending upon the situation. So knowing the word of God is important, in discerning if any of these words are actually coming through the Holy Spirit or the Spirit of the world.

We are told in 1 John to test the spirits, because not everything that comes out of the mouths of people is from God. A few times I have been listening to what may have been a great sermon, and there was just one thing that was said that did not seem to line up with the word of God. I would have to check it out, before I accepted what was said or rejected it.

So a word of knowledge can be something like. There is someone in this meeting that has some specific problem, that God desires to deal with. It could be sickness, financial, or maybe a problem they have with somebody else. The word is usually quite specific about the problem, but it is always down to the individuals free will to respond.

If a word of knowledge comes forth and it is not responded to, it is most probably because the person has some sort of fear regarding either the problem, or just in opening up and coming forward. The word has come forward because it is the right time for that problem to be dealt with.

If the word of knowledge comes alongside a word of wisdom, which will give a solution to the problem. Or a direction to take that will resolve the problem, or get you to start moving in the right direction by giving you steps to take. The word of wisdom could even be, what or how to pray about the problem.

There might even be a word of prophesy, that will let you know the outcome of following the words of knowledge and wisdom. If it comes through the holy Spirit, it is from God. If you do what the words are saying you will experience the solution. You will achieve the result that God has planned.

6 The gift of faith

**For we walk by faith, and not by sight
2 Corinthians 5:7**

Yes faith is a gift of the holy Spirit. This is the gift that shows that the gifts of the Holy Spirit are for everyday life. We do many things by faith without realising it sometimes. Then at other times we actively step out in faith. In fact every time you use a gift of the Holy Spirit you are acting in faith. Christianity is not a faith as such, that is a worldly way of looking at it. Within Christianity We have the gift of faith. This is such a big subject it could take up a whole book.

So faith comes by hearing, and hearing by the word of God. Romans 10:17

Much is said in the bible about the faith of Abraham. Why is Abraham lifted up as an example of faith? There many others too. Because he talked with God and believed words that God said. Even though he would not see the fulfilment of all that God promised to him. His faith was much stronger than any doubt.

God's word says that we are of the faith of Abraham. That is because we are the descendants of Abraham, as part of the promise made to him, to become the father of many nations. Abraham believed the promises of God, and it says that it was counted to him as faith.

**For by grace you have been saved through faith; and that not of yourselves, it is the gift of God
Ephesians 2:8**

Faith is a Spiritual gift. We have the gift of faith, it is supernatural. We begin our Christian life with faith given to us by God. The Spirit of God drew us to Him. It is nothing that we were able to do. We were supernaturally empowered with faith, to believe the word of God.

It seemed easy to accept Jesus as saviour at the beginning. For some reason after a while our faith begins to fade. We stop believing that God is able to work things in our lives, for our good. We begin to carry on in our own strength.

We forget the power that is within us. It is the power of God. This power comes through the Holy Spirit. This power is always with us, because Jesus said I will never leave you. Once the Spirit comes into us it will always be there. We can call upon that power whenever it is needed. It is within us.

Now to Him who able to do exceeding abundantly beyond all that we ask or think, according to the power that works within us. Ephesians 3:20

If our children are to live by faith in the Lord, they have to be able to see the example of this in their parents, or other significant adults in their lives. It is like this for all of us really. It is a fact of life, that we get infected, as it were by the attitudes around us. For instance when at work in an atmosphere of negativity, it is easy to begin to take on board the way that other people think.

This is called peer pressure. It can affect, and infect us as adults, just as much as it can affect, and infect our children. The antidote to this infection is faith. Faith is a gift from God. Instead of being infected by negativity, we can infect with faith. That is what we should be doing for the benefit of our children.

The world of business recognises this principle. Over the years I have been involved with some network marketing businesses. They all say the same thing, even if in different ways. If you want to be successful in the business, you have to mix with successful people. For this reason they Have big one day or weekend seminars. Being taught by the top successful people in that business. As they say Success breeds success. They understand how the mind works.

You can see that this is also the way that faith works. When you get around someone or a group of people that have an active faith. People that see God working in and through their lives, it becomes infectious. Faith breeds faith. Faith comes by hearing.

The opposite, with unbelief, is also true. So, if you get around people that are walking in faith, your faith gets stronger, and your unbelief becomes weaker. You can strengthen your faith though Prayer and fasting. As it says in Jude, praying in the Spirit, that is in tongues will build up you most Holy faith.

Unbelief can be a faith dampener, to put it mildly. Jesus had to deal with this in His disciples, after they could not heal the boy having convulsions. When Jesus said that this kind does not come out, but by prayer and fasting. He was not talking about the spirit in the boy, he was talking about the unbelief that they had and the faith that they needed. You could put it this way, 'This kind of faith does not come out but by prayer and fasting.'

They had faith, because they had been out healing the sick, casting out demons. Prayer and fasting builds your faith which in turn reduces your unbelief. Just like the disciples, you already have the power through the Holy Spirit. It is our faith that must get stronger than our unbelief. Or to put it the other way around. Our unbelief must become weaker than our faith. You just have to believe and not doubt.

And Jesus said to him, "'If you can!' All things are possible to him who believes." Immediately the boy's father cried out and began saying, "I do believe, help my unbelief." Mark 9:23-24

This shows that we can believe and also have unbelief at the same time. We have the gift of faith, but our mind, our experiences, or the words and atmosphere around us can cause us to also have unbelief. That is when we need the gift of the Spirit to rise up from within us, to defeat the spirit of unbelief. We can learn this, and so can our children. Faith is simple read what Gods word says and believe it! Because faith comes by hearing and hearing by the word of God.

7 Gifts of healing

This is perhaps, visibly the most wonderful gift. To lay hands on the sick and see them healed. Other gifts often go along side this gift. Words of wisdom and knowledge. These could be words that let you know why the person is sick, and how to pray or what to do. For instance, if the cause of the sickness is spirit, or a curse. This would be classed as a word of knowledge.

The word of wisdom would tell you how to deal with the problem. If we as adults exercised our faith and authority in dealing with sicknesses. Started talking to them and taking command over our own bodies to begin with. We would I am sure have more success in laying hands on and seeing other people healed.

Jesus told us that we should lay hands on the sick, and they *Will* be healed. We also have the power to cast out demons and raise the dead. It is not something that God will do, He told us to do these things. God will heal the sick if we do as He has instructed. He did not tell us to ask Him to heal. If we have the Holy Spirit, that is where the power flows through, to us. Jesus sent to us the Holy Spirit. He said When the Spirit comes you will receive power. According to the power that works within us.

Now to Him who is able to do far more abundantly beyond all that we ask or think, according to the power that works within us. Ephesians 3:20

I can do all things through Him who strengthens me. Philippians 4:13

It does not say that God can do all things through me, if He chooses to. The same Spirit that raised Jesus from the dead is within us. We have raising from the dead power. Can you believe that? Whether you believe it or not, Baptism in the Holy Spirit gives you that power. Whether you choose to use it or not. Look at it this way, someone might say to you that they don't believe in God. That does not mean that God does not exist. You have the Power. If you don't believe it, then you will not use the power. It does not matter if you believe or not You still have the power, to heal the sick raise the dead, and cast out demons.

I was not taught this as a child. I bet that most of you reading this were not taught these things as children. Jesus said we should have faith as a child. If you teach a child to lay hands on the sick and they will recover, they will believe it. We should teach this without doubt in our minds. Otherwise you will pass that doubt onto the child or children that you are teaching. We should also teach that if the person is not healed, that they should ask God for Knowledge and wisdom, about the reason. At the end of the day it is just plain and simple faith in what Jesus said,

These signs will accompany those who have believed; in My name they will cast out demons, they will speak with new tongues, they will pick up serpents, and if they drink any deadly poison it will not hurt them; they will lay hands on the sick and they shall recover. Matthew 16:17-18

In many places Jesus said that if you ask in My name it will be done. Ask without doubting. Believe that you have received when you ask, not when you see it. This is just simple faith. We are told that we should not doubt. When it comes to healing we should talk to the problem, not ask the Lord to heal, we are told to heal. Doubting and unbelief will not get the job done. As Jesus said, speak to the mountain, but do not doubt!

8 Effecting of miracles

Biblically miracles are different to healings. Most of the time Jesus preached the gospel and healed the sick. That was His ministry. Occasionally He performed miracles. So, what is a miracle? Generally speaking, it is a suspension of natural laws. There are Spiritual laws and there are natural laws. There is a reason for Paul to write about Healings and miracles. You could say that someone being healed is a miracle. Yes it is amazing, but it is a healing.

Raising someone from the dead is a miracle. It is a suspension or reversal of natural law. Other miracles that Jesus did were; turning water into wine, without brewing it. Walking on water, Calming the sea and the wind. Causing a mega catch of fish, feeding the 5000 plus people and more. You see that in all these cases and more, even those that occurred the old testament, it is the suspension of natural laws. If you look at it in this way, that a miracle is a temporary solution to a problem.

A miracle usually only lasts a short time, where a healing is for good. The longest miracle in the bible, is the feeding of the children of Israel with manna, for forty years in the wilderness. Once they got to the Promised land, and ate of its fruit, the miracle of the manna stopped. Also, the fact that the children of Israel's clothes and shoes did not wear out. Drinking, or ingesting a deadly poison and not being harmed is a suspension of natural law.

I have had some miracles happen in my life. Some odd things really, like stopping a washing machine from leaking just by praying. Praying over a car that suddenly stopped. Driving to somewhere in the pouring rain and commanding sunshine, then ten minutes later it was a beautiful day, until we got back into the car.

Just before I accepted Jesus as my Saviour I had broken the law for the third time doing the same thing and was for sure going to end up I prison. That is what everybody who knew anything about the law thought. I ended up not going to prison and got fined minimal amounts, much less than previous times for the same offences.

Something else that I might class as a miracle, is having broken my neck twice and surviving without any ill effects. The first time I did not even know that I had broken my neck, it showed up the second time as the doctors looked at my X-rays.

I remember one time, that I went to a three-day Christian conference for leaders of children's work. I had a minimal amount of money, enough to get there, pay towards the electric in the room and get some food to eat the first night.

In the last meeting of the conference, during the worship service, I was praying about how I was going to get home, a good two hundred miles, when somebody tapped me on the shoulder and handed me the money I needed to get from London to home. I still had to get to London, about one hundred miles. As I was walking out of the room of the meeting someone offered a ride to London with them in their car. They dropped me off at the bus station.

Miracles do happen!

9 Prophecy

The gift of prophecy is a marvelous gift, but the very nature of the word can be a source of misunderstanding. When we hear the word prophecy, the tendency is to think of the prophets of the old testament. Usually thinking of all the doom and gloom that was prophesied through them. This is understandable, there was so much prophesy that was of a curse like nature to much of what was said.

Even the prophesies about the future, our future. If you focus upon the bad things that are told about, that is going to happen, you will be of all people a gloomy soul. There are many of the prophecies in the books of the prophets that tell of the great and marvelous things that God has stored up for us. Like this one from Isaiah, talking about the result of the Messiah, Jesus fulfilling His work, creating a new covenant.

For this is like the days of Noah to Me; When I swore that the waters of Noah should not flood the earth again, so I have sworn that I will not be angry with you, nor will I rebuke you. "For the mountains may be removed and the hills may shake, but My lovingkindness will not be removed from you. And My covenant of peace will not be shaken," says the Lord who has compassion on you. Isaiah 54:9-10

Prophecy can be described as a direct word from God. It will never ever be contrary to the word of God as is written in the bible. It can be directed to a single person, or to a group of people. Prophecy is not all doom and gloom. There are different faces, or facets to prophecy. Yes, it can be the telling of future events. It can also be a word that guides you in what to do or say.

From my experience, prophecy is usually a word from God that is sent through the Holy Spirit, to build us up. A word that will encourage us in our faith. As the above prophecy from Isaiah. It may well be faith to do something that has been prayed about. Maybe a project that has been on the hearts of the body of believers.

Back when I was in my early twenties, I went to an event meeting at the evangelical church in my hometown. At the end of the service I went forward for prayer about the plans that God had for me. The visiting preacher had never met me before and did not know about any of the involvement that I had within my Baptist Church.

Prophesied over me that I would have much influence over children both for the Lord and in my life in general, for good. It was not until another twenty years that I became a swimming teacher. Though I was already involved in the teaching of children in the church. Every day I get the opportunity to share some part of my Christian faith to some of the children I work with at the swimming pool.

There is another aspect to prophecy, that I think has largely gone unnoticed, or unrecognised as prophecy. It is the use of our words, as the bible says blessing and cursing. The bible says that the words that we use are powerful. That is why it says, 'pray for you enemies, bless those who persecute you.' Every day that you speak a blessing over your children, or your spouse; anybody you come into contact with. You are prophesying a blessing upon them. Speak words of life to people, and you prophesy good towards them.

Death and life are in the power of the tongue, and those who love it will eat it's fruit Proverbs 18:21

James talks about the dangers of not controlling the words of our mouths. Our words are creative things. You know this and have experienced it in your lives. When someone criticises you or speaks other negative words to you. You get a little downcast, doubting yourself. Self-conscious. On the other hand, when we have words of encouragement spoken to us we become cheerful and positive. Words are important, and how we use them. If we speak Gods word, God's promise over ourselves, or our children, we prophesy to ourselves and our children. We prophesy God's blessing over ourselves.

If we follow God's word and only speak god's words of blessing over our children, they will learn to do the same over others. I know that sometimes you must correct and even chastise children, but it should be according to God's word of the new covenant, out of love and not anger.

10 Discerning of spirits

This gift normally or naturally goes along with the gift of prophecy, also with the gifts of wisdom, and knowledge. Everything that we hear and learn has come through the spiritual realm. The word of God talks about the wisdom of the world, which is usually opposed to the wisdom of God. When we get information given to us, or advice, we sometimes have to discern the spirit behind it. It might sound like good advice on the surface, but it leads us down the wrong path.

This is true of a lot of things that we learn. From the time that we are born till the end of our lives. Therefore, the gift of discerning of spirits is an essential part of the tools within the gifts of the Spirit.

But to those who are called, both Jews and Greeks, Christ the power of God, and the wisdom of God. Because the foolishness of God is wiser than men, and the weakness of God is stronger than men.
1 Corinthians 1:24-25

The use of the discerning of spirits within the gathering of the church is important as people can stand up and say things out of there heart, that may not be for everybody, or even from God. Also, some people can begin with a word from God, and not know when to stop. They continue talking (on in the flesh), not from God but from their selves.

It could be that they think that some explanation is needed, or that they feel that the word needs padding out. A lot of times a word that comes from God seems short and too simple. So it can get embellished. Discerning of the spirits is needed.

Discerning of the spirits is also of help when having to make choices about things in life. In the life of the church body, also in our personal lives. This gift as all the others can be utilised in our daily lives. Just think of the benefit it would be to lead you and your children in making right, choices according to the word of God. Being able to discern the spirit behind the things that face them, would enable them and us to make the right choices, and to walk by the Spirit and not in the flesh

I want you to think about and apply all of this, all the gifts of the Spirit to your children. Why would you not want the best for them. The best is all that God has, to give to them. It is for you; it is for your children. It is a gift from our Heavenly Father, to all who believe in the Name of the Lord Jesus Christ. Think of it like this. If a friend gave you a gift that was for another and asked you to give it on their behalf, and you decide to keep it for yourself, that would be stealing!

So, keeping the truth about the gift of the Holy Spirit, and the benefit of speaking in tongues from your children could be classed as stealing, at least being a stumbling block. Maybe that is why Jesus spoke about it being better to have a millstone around your neck and be drowned in the sea, for causing a child to stumble in their faith.

Think of the great benefit to children's lives to have the Holy Spirit with them all the time, guiding and teaching; giving them great wisdom in situations that they must deal with. If your children are believers, they have a God ordained right to receive the baptism in the Holy Spirit. It is not for us to decide for them and withhold the truth from them. That is, as I pointed out, stealing.

Think of it this way. You would not let your children go out in the pouring rain without the protection of a coat. So why would you let them go out into the world without putting on the Lord Jesus Christ, going out without the protection of the Holy Spirit. The Holy Spirit will lead them and guide them. It will teach them and give them wisdom in any of the circumstances they may find themselves in.

How would you feel, if when your child, or grandchild came home from school, and you asked them what they learned? They turn around and say not much, but Little Johnny fell over and cut his leg, so I prayed, and he was healed, what's for dinner?

It can happen if we teach our children the right things of the Kingdom of God. What about if the whole family came home in the evening and you sat round sharing the great things that God had done through you during the day. Marvelled at the way God was using you each day.

That is what happened in the early church. If we have the Baptism in the Holy Spirit, we have all the tools that we need to live a victorious life. To live a life that is led and empowered by the Holy Spirit. Us as adults sharing in the joy and power with our children.

The gift is for you and you and your children

Just imagine if all this manifestation of the gifts of the Holy Spirit were to work within the family unit. It can work in a family unit. The gifts of the Spirit are for the building up the body of Christ. Just because you are not at the church gathering, does not make you any less a part of the body. The gifts are for use every day, in your everyday lives.

This is probably something you have never heard before. Just think about it, meditate on it for a while. If they work for the family, and as you go about your daily life. Then when you meet at the church gathering, you can share what the Lord has been doing in your life. That helps to build up the rest of the body of Christ. That is a great reason to get used to using the gifts, all of the gifts of the Holy Spirit in our daily lives.

The gifts are for you and your children!

Chapter 7:
Religious Practices Verses Living Christianity

This could be a delicate subject. That is because I know that many people have grown up in churches where religious practices are the normal part of the way the church does things. I am not totally against some religious practices, because some of them are a necessary part of the living Christianity that I am going to be talking about. Again, this book is more about what we teach our children than anything else. We cannot teach children the things that we do not know ourselves

If you grew up going to a church that practiced unbiblical religious practices, it may be possible that you do not know the difference between what you follow and have come to accept, and the truth of the bible. For example, Christening has been adopted as baptism, where baptism means immersion, that is understood as total immersion, and should be done when a person accepts Jesus as their Saviour. More on this later in the Chapter.

If we were taught the wrong things as children, then later understand that they are wrong, why would you allow the wrong teaching to be passed on to your children? Could this be why young people walk away from church and Christianity? Is this why so many adults in our societies do not go to church, because they recognise the falseness and hypocrisy that exists within mainstream Christian denominations. It even happens within evangelical churches too. So how do we deal with this problem?

Surely the answer is in living a biblical way of life, the way that God wants us to live. Not our ideas or interpretations of how we think God wants us to live. We need to be more reliant upon God to meet our needs. Rather than rely upon our own efforts and gifts to get not only what we need, but also what we want. There are many promises of God in the bible that tells how God WILL prosper us in many ways. In every area of our lives, if we will live according to Gods plan, and not the worlds reasoning of how we should live.

The Lord will command the blessing upon you in your barns and all that you put your hands to. Deuteronomy 28:8

Many church organisations have adopted the worlds way of thinking within the things that they practice. Things put in place by the wisdom of man, Like the emphasis of obeying the Ten Commandments, rather than the wisdom of God. Sometimes things are adopted to try to make life easier, like set prayers. Restrictions on the length of church services. Things that actually, restrict God from being able to work as much or as effectively as He wishes. Things the restrict the working and power of the Holy Spirit. So, as we go into, and look at some of these practices, I ask you to keep an open mind, and test what I say and your views by the word of God.

See so it that no one takes you captive through philosophy and empty deception, according to the tradition of men, according to the elementary principles of the world, rather than according to Christ. Colossians 2:8

This scripture speaks specifically to the things that we do and follow within our churches. Things that have been adopted that are not according to the word of

God. Man's ideas that have been allowed to creep into our Christianity that can be classed as, 'Philosophy and empty deception, according to the tradition of men.'

I remember back in 1978 when I became born again. I was in the army, in the process of being discharged because I had been in trouble with the civilian police, borrowing a car without owners' consent. Sitting in the guardroom cell, I was visited by what they called an army Scripture Reader. He used to come and talk and leave Christian books to read. There was a book that I read and led me to the understanding that I need to receive Jesus as my Saviour.

The book was, 'The Cross and The Switch-blade.' After reading the book, I read the postscript written by Billy Graham, which said something like Nicky Cruz was the worst of the worst, if God can change Nicky's life He can change anyone. I know that I had not been as bad as Nicky, but knew that if God can help Nicky to change and get a better life, He can help me too.

I got the commander of the guardroom to phone the Scripture Reader. He left His dinner and came straight over, about an eight-mile journey. When he got to me, we talked for a while. Then we prayed and I accepted Jesus as my Saviour. Nothing great happened. There was no sudden revelation, that had already happened. I just had peace. A peace that I had not known before, knowing that I had done the right thing.

The next day I got permission to phone my mother, who I thought believed in God. After all she made sure that I went to Sunday School. This is what I remember saying to her, "Hi mum, I am getting thrown out of the army in two weeks, but everything is going to be alright, because I am a Christian now." Mum replied something like this, "Well we will see, if you keep the Ten Commandments."

When I got home two weeks later, my mum repeated the words she had said to me on the phone, "we will see if you keep the Ten Commandments." On the other hand, My Dad when he got home from work, picked me up by the throat, held me against the wall and said something along the lines of, "If you mention God, Jesus, or anything Christian in this house I will kill you." He was just upset that I had been thrown out of the army.

The thing about my story that I would like to point out is this. My mother thought that keeping the Ten Commandments made a person good enough to be classed as a Christian and get to heaven. That is what she was taught as a child, and that is how she saw Christianity at the age of over sixty.

If we teach children the wrong things, even if they are only slightly wrong, they believe that it is right, they believe that it is truth. Then if they continue in the church as adults being taught wrong how will they come to know the real truth, when they hear it? When they have respect and trust for the leader of their church who teaches something that is not the complete truth.

Traditions and Doctrines of Men

I have been thinking about things (religious practices) that we are told in the bible, that we have to do. I can come up with only two things that are required religious observances by the new testament church, we are the new testament church. Things that are a part of the new covenant. They are, the Lords Supper, or communion, and baptism. I know that some will say that we are told to, worship God, pray without ceasing; seek

God; preach the Gospel; heal the sick; raise the dead; cast out demons; love each other; love our neighbours, and many more things.

All of these are things that should be a part of every Christians everyday life. Baptism is a one-time occurrence in a Christians life. Twice if you count Christening. The lord's supper is a direct command from Jesus, "As often as you do this do it in remembrance of Me." There are no other days or festivals of religious observances that we are required or told in the bible to remember as new testament born again Christians.

Days such as Christmas, Easter, lent, Saints days, and any other day that are in the Christian calendar are things, that are traditions and doctrines of men. Some are to there make remembrance of certain things easier which is not necessarily a bad thing. When they become almost like a law to observe them, it at the least weakens the freedom from the law of sin and death that Jesus won for us. At worst it puts us back under the bondage of a law that should never be there in the first place.

If we teach children these wrong practices they will not know that they are wrong. They will believe that they are right, because so much of the Christian world recognises these things. The verse in proverbs that says, train a child up in the way he should go, and he will not depart from it even when he is old, is true even if when we teach them wrong things, wrong ways. They will stick to them all their life, whether the practices are good or bad.

This has become a big problem with a lot of adult Christians. We have grown up into wrong teachings, and ways of doing things. So much to the point that they will reject outright even some of the basic principle truths of the Christian faith. Such as having to be born again, actually, accepting Jesus as saviour, then to be baptised. Instead of assuming Jesus is your saviour, assuming, that you are saved, and will go to heaven.

That is the way much of the modern Christian world thinks. God has forgiven sin in the world. We don't need to do anything, except follow His commandments. That is living with the old covenant, negating the death of Jesus.

The old covenant works like this. There are blessings for keeping the law. Some amazing blessings, but there are also some real bad curses for breaking the law. Under the law of God if you commit adultery you should be stoned to death. So how many of us should still be living if we walked according to the law. God's word says that if you are living according to the law, then break the tiniest little bit of the law, then you are guilty of breaking the whole law. So, it is not about just keeping the Ten Commandments. Here is a very strong statement.

Because the mind set on the flesh is hostile towards God; for it does not subject itself to the law of God, for it is not even able to do so. Romans 8:7

There are so many things that come under this topic that I could not cover them all. I will just cover some of the main things. Again, it is not an attack on what anybody believes and practices some of these things, but hopefully an enlightenment upon the truth and how things ought to be. Words are important, the words we speak and, also the words we sing. Sometimes we just say or sing things without any thought to what is coming out of our mouths. Words are important enough for God to tell us that,

"Death and life are in the power of the tongue."
Proverbs 18:21

<u>Crosses</u>

I was in a Pentecostal church on Sunday morning in 2018. One of the pastors an elderly man requested that we sing his favorite song. 'The Old Wooden Cross.' The words came up on the screen. I read them and instantly knew in my spirit that I could not sing this song. I wrote this note in the bible app on my phone, 'The song, 'The Old Wooden Cross, is idolatrous. This song is worship of the Cross. Yes, the sentiment of the song is that it is the cross of Jesus the Saviour, but it is worship of the cross and not of Jesus, or God the Father.

This song turns the cross into an object of worship, an idol. I know that there are many who love that song, and that I will be stepping on many peoples toes. Not just about the song but what I have to say about crosses, some people have them hung around their necks and use them, or trust them, like they are lucky charms. In moments of anguish or hearing some bad news they touch the cross or even rub it with fingers.

I am not against wearing crosses, as an identification of your faith, I used to wear one, but they are not lucky charms. A lucky charm is an idol! A cross around your neck does not provide protection from anything in the Lord or otherwise. The same is true about Saint Christopher pendants. Yet we teach children that they do provide protection. This is wrong.

So, talking about crosses as idols. The ones that some churches have hung up on the walls within the churches, they can and have become types of idols, in a real sense. Some have a supposed image of Jesus on them, some are just an empty cross. Some churches require that you kneel before the cross before you sit down in the pews. Or make the sign of the cross in front of you as you enter. As a sign of reverence before God, as you enter into worship.

Nowhere in scripture are we told to do this. It is Worship and Praise that brings us into the presence of God. A cross should not be something to pray before or pray to, because it then is in danger of becoming an object of worship.

Therefore, let us draw near with confidence to the throne of grace. Hebrews 4:16

We have confidence because we know that we are forgiven, for all our sin, past present and future. God will not hold any sin against us. The devil will. Our hearts will, as we feel that we are not worthy. The truth is we are not worthy, but Jesus died that we would become worthy enough to be called sons of God. And so, in Jesus we are now worthy.

I think That Crosses should only be on the outside of church buildings, for the reason they were put there in the beginning. So that people know and recognise that it is a place of worship of our God and Father of the Lord Jesus Christ. Decorating the inside of a worship building is not a subject that I wish to debate. But it is just a place that we the Church join together to worship our God. It does not matter if man has consecrated it, or it is considered Holy ground. People of God can worship anywhere. In a home, a field, a town square. You do not need a consecrated building.

For we are the temple of the living God; just as God said, "I will dwell in them and walk among them. 2 Corinthians 6:16

Some people even have them same attitude for 'the' church building. Yes it is a place that has been consecrated for the worship of God, but the church building is not where God resides. When we go to the building God is there because we take Him there with us. The word says the we are the temple of God. He resides within us. So that wherever we go He is with us. Jesus said that He and the Father will come and live in us. That is the Holy Spirit. God the Father, God the Son, and God the Holy Spirit. The three are one, the Holy Trinity.

Do you not know that you are the temple of God, and the Spirit of God dwells in you.
1 Corinthians 3:16

This is truth, we are Holy because God made us Holy. He placed His righteousness. Within us. God promised:

"I will never leave you nor forsake you.
Hebrews 13:5

Then we have to know, who we are in Christ Jesus. Know what He has given to us and walk in the faith of that knowledge. Then we will be able to teach our children to walk in the same manner. If you do not know that you are the temple of God. And free from the law, (power) of sin and death **Romans 8:2** We cannot train our children up in the right way, in truth. We are blind leading the blind. If we stumble they will stumble.

Praying – (set prayers)

And when you are praying, do not use meaningless repetition as the gentiles do, for they suppose that they will be heard for their many words.

Matthew 6:7

Praying has been mis-taught for years, maybe hundreds or thousands of years, in many parts of the Christian church. Set prayers, prayers that get repeated over and over word for word can and do become meaningless. There are many set prayers, such as hail Mary's, to bedtime prayers we have learned to say with our children. Even saying grace over our food. Prayers that are just said from memory, and have no real meaning or power.

Let's start with 'The Lord's Prayer' Jesus never said, when you pray, pray these words. To call it the Lord's prayer I think is an error to start with, because Jesus never prayed these words. Jesus said pray like this, in this way. The prayer shows us in what manner we should be praying. And that, if we are living according to the old covenant, of the law of sin and death. The start of it shows us to begin by worshiping God Coming into the presence of God. Have we not already done this by our praise and worship in the meeting (service)?

The next part is an acceptance of Gods will here on earth, more than that, to command His will here on earth, then is another command to God, that we have food to sustain us. After this we are shown that we call upon, tell God to forgive us of our sin, it will only work if you have forgiven all others that sin against you.

This is old covenant praying, because after the death and resurrection of Jesus, our sin is already forgiven. In truth we should be thanking Him for forgiving us of our sin. Because in Jesus death, the sins of the whole world are already forgiven.

The next bit is old covenant also, lead us not into temptation. In the old covenant yes God used to test

His people allow them to be tempted. We do not need to ask or Tell God to lead us not into temptation under the new covenant. This because we cannot be tempted by God only by ourselves and our minds, our way of thinking, and by the devil.

Let no one say when he is temped, "I am being tempted by God"; for God cannot be tempted by evil, and He Himself does not tempt anyone. But each one is tempted when he is carried away and tempted by his own lust. James 1:13-14

God will not deliver us from the evil one, as He told us to do it. In James God says to resist the devil and he will flee from us. God can give us the wisdom to help us to resist the devil, but he has already given us the authority to do it. People in the old covenant did not have this authority. The devil no longer has authority over us, to lead us away from God, because he is defeated. The only time that the devil gains authority over us is when we allow him to.

Then the end of the "Lord's prayer" is to give God the glory, More worship and praise. The Lord's prayer is a pattern for prayer, a way to pray. A formula for prayer. That is for people living under the covenant of the law. Jesus told us as His friends that we can ask anything in His name, and He will do it. Even better than that, we have direct access to God.

A side note to this "Lord's prayer" is that it does not ask God for anything. It seems that there is a pattern for commanding God. This may come as a shock to some of you, even sound blasphemous.

There is another scripture a command from God Himself to back up this idea of us commanding God. A truth that I have only come to realise and understand within the last year of writing this. It is to do with praying according to the will of God. This is what God tells us to do according to the works of His hands. According to His will. If we pray according to his will, he has given to us the authority to command His will.

Thus, says the Lord, the Holy One of Israel, and his maker, "Ask Me of things to come concerning My sons and the work of My hands, you command Me." Isaiah 45:11

Other set prayers I think are mainly Catholic, like Hail Mary's. We are only supposed to be Praying to God the father, in the name of Jesus. We are not supposed to be praying to dead people asking them to petition for us to the Father. Jesus does that, and you better know that He does, He knows the right way to pray for us. He always gets His Prayers right. So, we should not be praying to Mary, or the 'Saints', or anybody else. Jesus said many times ask the Father in My name. We Have access straight to the throne of God, because Jesus made the way for us.

For through Him (Jesus) we both have our access in one Spirit to the Father. Ephsians2:18

There is now NO condemnation for those who are in Christ Jesus. Romans 8:1

So, we do not have to fear God because we did something wrong. We do not have to go through a mediator because we have become unworthy to approach God. God will not condemn you. He is waiting with arms open to receive us. He sees us in the spirit which has been redeemed, washed as white as snow. God promised that He will never be angry at us.

So, I have sworn that I will not be angry with you. Nor will I rebuke you. For the mountains may be removed, and the hills may shake, but My lovingkindness will not be removed from you, and My covenant of peace will not be shaken, say the Lord who Has compassion on you. Isaiah 54:9-10

So, we do not need an intermediary, to pray on our behalf, why then do churches have confessionals where the people go to have their confessions heard by the priest? God through Jesus is the one who forgives sin.

For there is one god, and one mediator between God and men, the man Christ Jesus. 1 Timothy 2:5

If we sin against any person we should go to that person to ask for their forgiveness. God has already forgiven us. God does not want that we should be indebted to anyone else or have anyone indebted to us. That is why Jesus said if while you are making an offering and remember that you or your brother have something against one or other, go settle the dispute first.

Why is this? It is because unforgiveness can be a thing that comes between you and God. It can open up the door to Your enemy who seeks to devour anybody who will give him the chance. Remember this though, Gods love continues to flow towards us, in a constant flow. Unforgiveness can hinder you from receiving that which you want to receive.

Therefore, confess you sins to one another, and pray for one another, so that you may be healed. The effective prayer of the righteous man can accomplish much. James 5 16

This verse is not talking about praying for healing, it just says to pray for one another, because if you don't, you block the flow of God to heal you. These are things that we ought to be teaching our children. Not just to say sorry to someone they have wronged, but to ask for forgiveness also. That they should forgive when they are wronged.

The scripture above from James especially if you add the read verse 14, and 15, indicate that not confessing your sin to each other and asking forgiveness from the person that you sinned against, can cause sicknesses to come upon you.

Before I finish this section on praying, I must mention two of the sorriest prayers that people say and teach their children. The first one is the bedtime prayer, 'now I lay me down to sleep, I pray the Lord my soul to keep. If I die before I wake I pray the Lord my soul to take.'

This is an unbeliever's prayer, full of uncertainty, because it says that they don't know that they are saved by the blood of the Lord Jesus. They do not know that God is already keeping their souls. They do not know that God has given angels charge over them. They do not believe in the Lord Jesus Christ. They do not know if they will go to heaven or hell. They do not know if they will even wake up! It is a prayer just in case!

I know that I will wake up in the morning. I know because God has work for me to do. He will not let my life end until He has completed what He began in me. In Jeremiah God says that we will have an expected end. That says to me that he will let me know when His work for me is done, and it is time to leave this temporal body.

We should teach children to pray something like this, "Thank you father God for the good day I had today, thank now for my time of rest, strengthen me as I sleep, that I may wake up refreshed in Your Spirit, ready for the day ahead." This is more like a prayer of faith.

The second prayer, that is a prayer of unbelievers is the saying of grace over their food. It goes like this. 'For what we are about to receive may the Lord make us truly Thankful.'

Firstly, if you are not thankful for the food you are about to eat, then God will not, and cannot do anything to make you thankful. Secondly as with the above bedtime prayer it is meaningless. Why would anybody pray such a meaningless prayer as this? Thank God for the food, bless the person who prepared the food, bless the food and ask that it nourish and sustain you until next time you eat. This is a more appropriate prayer over your food.

Let's teach children to pray the right way. Encourage them to use their own words, not meaningless repetition. Encourage them to listen to The Holy Spirit, and pray as the Spirit leads. Prayers that mean something to them and to God. Teach them to Pray in faith, not uncertainty. If they know the promises of God for them and us all, they will know how to pray in faith. Adding, "If it be your will oh God." Is turning the prayer into a prayer of unbelief

While on the subject of prayer, let me just mention a couple of other things that we are taught to do. Things that are not Always necessary. Bowing heads, kneeling to pray, and putting hands together while praying, closing their eyes to pray. I know that none of these things are wrong, but to teach that you **have** to do them is wrong. But why not teach them also, that they can lift up their eyes, walk around praying. Teach them to lift up their hands to God, Lay on the floor before God. These are all good and biblical ways for praying.

Yes, I know that closing your eyes can and will help you to focus on the Lord, and cut off distractions around you. Help to listen for the leading of the Spirit in your Prayers, but God will hear your prayer eyes open or shut. You can't close your eyes while praying as you walk down the street. Or while driving your car. Or doing anything that you need to see with your eyes. Then again maybe you don't pray at any of these times! Why not? God's word says,

Pray without ceasing 1 Thessalonians 5:17

If your children are baptised in the Holy Spirit, they then can learn that they can speak in tongues, and should be encouraged to pray in tongues, as often as they pray, and more often. If we pray in tongues it is impossible to not pray according to Gods will. It can also bring revelation, (words of knowledge or wisdom), about how or what to pray.

Going to Church

Why do we go to church? This may seem like a stupid question to most. Here are some suggestions of reasons people go to church. You will recognise some of them, some of the things you might say really! It is a fact that everybody who goes to church have their reasons for going, but not all the reasons are the right reasons.

1 To worship God.

This may seem obvious. It is a good reason for attending church. How often do you worship God though? Is it only on Sunday when you go to church? This is not right. We should be worshiping God every day. Worship of God should be a part of our every day Christian life, not a once a week, Sunday experience. That is setting a bad example to our children. They need to know, and understand, that they can worship God anytime, anywhere, any day. We go to the church gathering to worship with our brothers and sisters in Christ. It should be an extension of what we are already doing within our daily lives

2 To fulfil a weekly Christian duty.

This is a purely religious act. It has absolutely no worth attached to it. It is an act of law. Or even an act of wanting to be seen as a church going person, not something that is done through faith, out of love for God. Many of us grow up being taught this attitude, then feel guilty if we miss a week. Taught that If we don't go to church that God will not be pleased with us.

This is a lie. God is more likely to be displeased because we go to church for the wrong reasons. You go to church because that is what you think God says you should do. No He does not. God say's you should gather as a church to encourage one another and build each other up.

And let us consider how to stimulate one another to love and good deeds, not forsaking our own assembling together, as is the habit of some, but encouraging one another; all the more as you see the day drawing near. Hebrews 10:24-25

God says that you should do everything out of the love that he has placed inside of you. You love God so you go to worship Him. God does not love you any more or less, whether you go to church every week or not. I would have to say that going to church for even the wrong reasons is better than not going at all. At least it is an opening for God to actually speak to you. It is just a question of whether you have your ears on. Being open to hear what God has to say.

I read and hear God speak to me every day. I don't have to go to Church for this. I go to Church to be encouraged and built up in the Lord, and to encourage and build other people up. We are being built up together as a part of the body of Christ. As Peter puts it, "we are as living stones."

3 To fellowship with friends.

This is a great reason to go to church, Gods word says, "do not neglect meeting together." As I have said already, by fellowshipping with each other, we can encourage one another and build each other up. This is the right reason for meeting with other believers. This is a great example to set before our children.

But if the only reason you go to fellowship is to catch up on the latest gossip of what is going on with people in the church, or the neighborhood, it is a bad reason, and so wrong. The right reason for fellowship would be to show love for people and even be someone who can help others that may be in some kind of need.

Rejoice with those who rejoice, and weep with those who weep. Be of the same mind toward one another; do not be haughty in mind but associate with the lowly. Do not be wise in your own estimation. Romans 12:15-16

4 To confess your sins or ease you conscience.

Is this a good reason to go to church? I think not, and I will explain why I think this. If you have been sinning all week long since the last time you went to church, there is something wrong with your religion. You are actually making it religion, a religious act, instead of a living faith. Especially the thought that 'It is done for one week; I can get on with my normal sinful life until next week.'

You may not actually think this way, but you are, by living this way. You have made the choice to live a sinful life. This is probably the worse example that parents can set for their children. Why not make the choice to live a Godly life.

In any case, if you feel the need to confess your sins, God will hear you at any time. You do not have to go to church. Nobody is perfect yet; we are in the process. We cannot live without some sort of sin knocking at our door. We must resist. Myself, if I find that I have a wrong thought come into my head and I do not to rebuke it straight away. I will, at the time that I realise that this has gone too far, Will say, "Sorry Lord I repent." I don't have to wait until I get to church on Sunday. Nobody has to wait until Sunday to repent!

As I have said before, God does not reside in a church building, He is alive in me. Wherever I go He is with me. It is the same for you too. God Lives in you, as I have already shown. This is something that is vitally important to teach children. Emmanuel – God with us is not something that is just for Christmas. It is something to remember every day You don't need to go to church to confess your sins. You should be more of the mind to go to church to rejoice that you have been forgiven. Even this can be done anytime anywhere.

5 Weddings and Funerals

I would guess that this is one on the main reasons that non-believers end up going to church. The thought that I have in my mind is that non-believers should not be getting married in church. You may think that I am wrong, but it is just a thought. I know that if you have the opportunity to get non-believers into church, that it is an opportunity to preach the gospel to them.

This rarely happens during a wedding ceremony. Another question is, if a person does not believe in God Why would they want to get married in a church, have a Christian wedding? It has become a tradition of man that nullifies the power of the gospel.

This is more of a religious observance than an act of faith. I do know that a lot of people do not get married in church, also many choose not to get married at all. When I was growing up it seemed to be every girl's dream to get married in church.

To walk down the aisle, in their wedding dress. Weddings have become big business, too commercial, just as Christmas. Is this why some churches will marry non-believers, for the money? Or is it more to do with political correctness, in that someone everybody has a right to get married in a church, whether they believe or not.

This is the wisdom, or thinking of the world, rather than from God. It is a way that the enemy the devil has been able to influence the minds of people, in the effort to dilute the truth of the word of God, and the Christian faith. Everyone should not have the right to get married in the church. That is a bold statement I know, but it is the truth.

Much of what I have said about weddings is also true about funerals, words are said about a hope for a future life for the dead person, The resurrection. When most of the people in attendance know that, that person was not a believer in the Lord Jesus Christ. That they will not be in Heaven. By reason of ignorance they think that maybe the person will make it to Heaven. Because deep down they were a good person, that helped a lot of people. But Jesus said that no one will see the Kingdom of God unless they become born again.

6 Christenings.

Before I begin talking about Christenings, I have to say that, I know that there are those who are true believers in the Lord. That will want to have, or already have Christened their children and are living in the best way they know how to fulfil the requirements, to raise their children in the way of the Lord. That they have chosen wisely to have God parents who are also believers.

This is not a criticism of those people. Or of anyone really. It is just to show the difference between the worldly way of looking at infant baptism, against the Christian view. That it has become more of a tradition and doctrine of man, than an act of faith.

The idea for christenings is taken from the Jewish tradition of presenting a new-born child to the Lord at the temple, at eight days old. This is where the child was named, circumcised, and dedicated to the Lord. The act of circumcision was to identify the child as a part of the covenant made with Abraham. As a part of the nation of Israel.

So, someone in the church decided it would be a good idea to have a Christian ceremony for babies, that reflected the old testament law, this Jewish ritual. All except for circumcision, which was no longer a requirement under the new covenant.

This all seems good, as long as the parents of the babies being Christened were believers. Even God parents could seem like a good idea, because if the parents died, while the child was still young; the Godparents could continue to raise the child in the Christian faith.

Somewhere along the line all the good reasons for the ceremony of Christening has been lost. It has become for the most, just a religious ceremony that has not a lot to do with the Christian faith. Yes, all the right things may be said, and promises made to raise the child according to the Christian faith. On the whole most of the parents and God parents do not believe in the Lord at all, so really they are lying.

To a lot of people, a Christening is just another excuse to have a party. I know this because I used to be a mobile DJ and was employed to provide music for quite a few Christening celebrations. Here is a truth that may shock some, but if you are a true believer you know already.

'Being Christened does not make you a Christian.'

We should be teaching children the right reasons for going to church. When I am in church it saddens me to see children in church who have been given things to occupy them while the adults' worship. Things like phones, iPads, even colouring books, and non-Christian books to read. As churches we should be doing more to engage the children, all the children in the worship. I am not just talking about songs aimed at children here.

If an adult was to be seen on an iPad or phone playing a game, or texting, eyebrows would be raised, as the very least. I have seen it even when they are reading the bible on their device. Yet children are allowed because they are children. The worship goes on in ignorance, instead of encouraging the children to join in. This not teaching children the importance of worship.

7 Reading the Bible

I can hear you asking, "How can reading the bible not be a good thing?" Well generally speaking reading the bible is a good thing. At least you are giving God the opportunity to speak to you from His word. But there is are wrong ways or reasons for reading the bible. I used to do one of them myself. I am sure that if I did this, there are many others who did, and maybe some who still do this. Reading the bible as like it was a daily chore. Something to be done, and got out of the way with, so you can get on with your day.

This is why I do not really like these verses of the day things. I do get verses of the day on my bible app on my phone, but usually I will read the whole chapter, unless Gods stops me and speaks to me about a particular verse. Which He often does. Then I write down the thoughts that I come into my mind on that verse. Yes, the verses of the day are good, to get you to even just open your bible and read, but if it is done with the attitude of, I need to read My verse of the day, before I get on with what I have to do, then it is the wrong reason. It can become just a religious act.

It is true that God can speak to us though this. Most of the time we read, then meditate on it for a few minutes. Then it is put to the back of our minds, as we have more important things to get on with. Nothing can be more important that sewing the seed of God's word into your heart.

The opposite to this is, that we read too much in one go that we do not retain any of what we read. This can happen when we follow reading plans, such as reading the bible in a year. Again, I am not against this. The point that I make is this. We can get so caught up in making sure, that we keep up the regime of reading enough chapters, that we can miss it when God wants to say something to you about a particular verse.

It can happen like this. You begin your reading of daily chapters, you get halfway through the first chapter, and you get a thought, 'I did not notice that before.' You think about it for a minute, make a mental note, then continue to read your daily quota.

By the time you have finished reading your quota for the day, the mental note you made forty minutes before has vanished. That thought way back in the first chapter could have been the Holy Spirit guiding you to look at that verse a bit deeper. Even to only take in and study what that verse was saying. Now because you did not take notice of the leading of the Spirit, you have missed What God was trying to speak to you. Why because you were so focused on the religious practice of reading through the whole bible in a year, and not actually upon what God is saying.

Another reason that is wrong, a reason some people read the bible, is for ammunition. There are a few reasons people do this. Mainly to prove to other people that they are wrong. Sometimes it is to find a reason not to believe in God! I have heard people say that they won't believe because the bible contradicts itself. It is a fact that if you look hard enough for what you are looking for you can make it sound contradictory. Just placing the Old covenant of the law, against the new covenant of grace. It can seem like a contradiction. I don't want to teach on that. It is just that reading the bible for this reason is wrong.

I have seen it and experienced it to where a spouse uses the word to prove the other person wrong, using the word of God against a person is wrong use of the word. This is what the devil does, he did it to Jesus, so why would he not use someone to do it to you too. We should be using the word of God to encourage and build each other up, not tear down the other person.

The right reasons to read the bible are to learn the truth, to build yourself up in the truth, and faith. To allow God to speak to you through His word. Knowing what God is really like, so you can use it to help other people. The number one way for God to speak to us His children is through His word, the bible. This is what we should be teaching our children.

That by reading the word of God, we get to know the mind of God. We get to know what God's will is. How can we pray according to God's will if we don't know it by reading Gods word, allowing God to speak to us through His word.

8 Taking the name of the Lord in vain.

I find that the biggest objectors to the way people talk and use the name of God like a swear word, are religious people. They take great offense at people you cry out 'Jesus' for no apparent reason except not to swear. It is not right to become offended at a person for this reason. It shows what the state of their heart is. It also shows what God says about there not being an excuse for anybody not to know that He exists.

When someone says, 'Oh God' or 'Jesus', I normally ask the person if they are praying. If they say no I then tell them that I think, that every time someone calls out the name of God or Jesus, I can imagine God tilting His ear to listen to what that person has to say. Or I will say, "Praise the Lord, you are praying." When they ask if I am religious, I tell them no, I am a child of the living God, Jesus is my Saviour. When someone takes the name of the Lord in vain, I see as an opportunity to witness the love of God to them. Not chastise them. That is the way that I think.

Have you ever thought about this, especially when something goes wrong, People call out the name God, Or Jesus. They never say Oh Allah, Buddha, or Mohamed, or any other so-called god. It is, I think, a testimony to Who is the real and living God. As the word of God say's,

For since the creation of the world His invisible attributes, His eternal power and divine nature, have been clearly seen, being understood through what was made, so they are without excuse Romans 1:20

All of these things that I have spoken of in this chapter are things that we should be teaching our children. The right way, the right reasons. The truth that is written in God's word, not the religious practices, and ideas. If you want children to believe what is false, then carry on teaching them the wrong things, man's ideas, rather than the truth.

The truth brings life, it lights the path that we should be walking. Not doing things simply because that's the way it has always been done, because that is a lie. Things have been done in the wrong way since somebody, a human being, decided that this is how we are going to do things. Maybe because it is seemed easier, or a good idea at the time, rather than to do things Gods way.

Many of us grew up having learned all of these wrong ideas about being a Christian. I thought I was a Christian because I was from a Christian country, until I became born again. I was under the impression that if I did not get married in church it was not right in God's eyes. I thought that if I read some bible every now and again it was good in God's view.

I thought that if I prayed every now and again, it was sufficient for god to hear me, especially when I really needed Him. I was under the impression that because I had been Christened I was a Christian. I thought that going to church once a month was pleasing to God. I did not know anything about living a Christian life, until after I accepted Jesus as my saviour.

Even after I became a Christian there were still people telling me these same things. These were all things that I learned as I grew up. They are subtle lies of the devil, designed to prevent people from realising the truth of the gospel. We should be teaching our children the truth, not the deceptions that have become a part of our Christian culture.

I looked at a survey on Christianity, which said that in the United Kingdom only five percent of the population goes to church regularly, only something like thirty-eight percent believe in God. We are not a Christian nation, we are not a multicultural nation, we are a multi-religious society. That has had to become politically correct in order to protect different peoples from Objecting to the truth of the Gospel. More than that, to protect the Gospel from objecting to the anti-Christian views of the peoples.

**Jesus said, "I the way, the truth and the life, and no one come comes to the Father but through Me."
John 14:8**

We need to make the biblical Christians views on everything in life, bigger than the worlds religious views, within our children.

Chapter 8: Psychology

Death And Life Are In The Power Of The Tongue. Proverbs 18:21

You may be wondering or asking why there is a chapter on psychology in a Christian book? A good question, but psychology affects everyone of us, whether you believe it or not. It may not be psychology as the world sees it, with its outcomes, but there is psychology in all aspects of our lives.

It does not matter whether you are a Christian or not. That is why there is a booming industry in self-help books for everything from business to sports. Psychology has become a big business, because even the world can see the effect that words can have on people and the way they think about themselves.

Your psychology has developed over all the years of your life. Mainly as a child. Especially the way you think about yourself. The way that you think about yourself has developed over your growing years, from the day of your birth. As I said earlier in this we begin to learn from birth, we continue to learn until we die.

The way that we think about ourselves, is a reflection of largely what has been said to us, or about us, as we were growing up. This is from a combination of sources. from parents, siblings, and other children. Even things seen on the television, internet and magazines.

Every time that someone said a negative thing about you it becomes a curse. The bible speaks so much about the use of words. About how we should use them. We should not call someone a fool, or idiot. We should not say to anyone, "You are useless." Or "can't you do anything right?" these are curses. And if you receive them, you receive the curse of those words. That will become how you will think about yourself. As children we are not taught how to combat these things, these words. Then we carry them into adulthood, and they still haunt us.

But no one can tame the tongue; it is a restless evil and full of deadly poison. With it we bless our Lord and Father; and with it we curse men, who have been made in the image of God; from the same mouth come both blessing and cursing. My brethren these things ought not to be this way. James 3:8-9

Even now as adults, we are molded by what other people say and think about us. People around us, the people that we associate with. They say things that that reinforce the way we feel about ourselves. Strengthen any insecurities that we may have. They might not know that they are doing this. They are ignorant of the things that you try to keep hidden deep inside. All of these things that we hold on to, keep buried inside. We hope that nothing happens or is said that will raise them up to the surface.

The truth is that we have been set free from all of these curses that were spoken over us from our childhood. We have been set free from every curse that has ever been spoken over us. There is no longer any reason to feel condemned, ashamed, or even confused by these things. Jesus was made a curse for us

There are curses that are written down in the Old Testament. Curses for not obeying the Law, the Law of sin and death. Jesus came and fulfilled the law. Nobody else managed to do that, the bible says that is impossible for anyone to fulfill the law. But Jesus the Son of the God who created the law, fulfilled all the requirements of the law.

He did this on our behalf, He became a curse for us, He took all the curses for breaking the law upon himself. Now we are free from all the curses of the law. A lot of those curses were either death, or sickness. It names them, and there is also this verse

Also every sickness and every plague which, not written in the book of this law, the Lord will bring on you until you are destroyed. Deuteronomy 28:61

So this curse included sicknesses and plagues that were not even discovered yet, like cancer, and aids...... The point is, these are the words of God. God spoke them. God spoke both the blessing and the curse. Jesus set us free from this law of sin and death, the law of the curse, into the law of the Spirit of life in Christ Jesus. **Romans 8:2**

So there is no more reason to feel ashamed, confused or condemned. You are free, but maybe you don't feel it. Maybe you were abused in some way verbally, mentally or physically. These are all curses. It all goes to build up your psychological profile.

Hopefully we will be able to counteract some of those things. In the process learn how to talk to our children in the right way, and not allow these same problems to affect them in their lives. Learn how to build up confidence within them and not negativity. Use words for a positive effect, because words are a powerful force to us all. If you do not believe this, then you are denying the truth. God created all things by the power of His word. Words have creative power, either for good or for bad. Yes even our words.

That is what God says in His word, it is what Jesus said, "If you have faith the size of a grain of mustard seed, You will SAY to this mountain….…." Many times it takes you, the person who is under the oppression of the curse to actually say to the curse. "By the blood of Jesus I am free from this curse (whatever it is)."

You have the authority, and the power to rebuke any curse spoken over you. Your own words are more powerful than any word spoken against you. You have to believe this and teach your children this also. Plus you have the authority of the Father, the son and the Holy Spirit. What I am trying to show you is the power of words. Words you hear, read, and say.

When I was younger about thirty-five plus years ago, I read some books on child psychology. One of the most impressionable things that I remember from those books was this. For every negative thing said to a child, it will take ten positive assertions said to the child, to counteract the negative.

Now that is a lot of work of positiveness, just to restore the balance of a child's self-worth, over one wrong thing said. Is it not better to say things in the right way to start with. You can build people up with your words, this is what this chapter is about. You can also build yourself up with your words and the word of God.

I work with children of all ages still, as a swimming teacher, and a diving coach. It amazing the amount of children that say to me, "I can't do it, I'm useless." Then I have to explain to them in various ways, that it is a learning process. Some things we learn quick at, and some things take more time. Even some children say something like, "It's no good, I will never get it."

The truth is, It is just time and practice. This is the same with everything that we learn to do in our lives. As long as we do not give up. Giving up reinforces the feeling of inadequacy that we have. It is just one more thing that says to our subconscious mind that we are not good enough. We can't make it; we will never achieve.

It is a true statement that we are not worthy to come into the presence of God. Trouble is we get taught this from Gods word, by the leaders of a lot of churches. The thing is, that this statement is only part of the truth. We are not worthy by our own efforts. There is nothing that we can do to become worthy enough to enter into Gods presence. We can humble ourselves; confess every sin we can think of; we can work tirelessly for the church; we can do all we can to help people, but nothing is enough to earn worthiness to be in God's presence. As the Apostle Paul wrote:

And if I give all my possessions to the poor, and if I surrender my body to be burned, but do not have love, it profits me nothing. 1 Corinthians 13:3

Here is another true statement. Through Jesus Christ, the Son of God, we have been made worthy enough to be able to enter into the presence of God. It is not something that we were able to do. It is something that God did, because He wants for us to be able to have a relationship with Him. It is God's desire for us to come into His presence. He made us righteous by placing His righteousness within us. He gave to us the faith of Jesus.

This is for you and your children.

For Paul also says this:

And may be found in Him, not having a righteousness of my own, derived from the law, but that which is through faith in Christ, the righteousness which comes from God on the basis of faith. Philippians 3:9

God is well pleased

We have to understand what God say's about us, not what we think about ourselves. Just think about that for a while, 'What Gods say's about us.' This what god said about Jesus after He was baptised, "This is My beloved Son, in whom I am well pleased." Jesus had not begun His ministry yet, had not overcome the temptations of the devil. He had not performed any miracles or healings. Yet. God said this about Him, after Jesus was baptised.

Just imagine if everyone who was baptised heard the audible voice of God saying, "You are my beloved son in whom I am well pleased." Would that take away all doubt in your mind that you are righteous enough to enter into the presence of God? It is by faith you are saved; it is by your faith that God is pleased with you.

This is what we are declaring to all who are present at our baptism, 'We are sons of God.' We should know and believe this. God is well pleased when we are baptised! Just because you do not hear the audible voice of God say it, does not make it any the less true. God is always well pleased when we follow His Son Jesus' example.

Jesus said, "Do the things that I did and greater things than these." When we do the things that Jesus did, God is well pleased. God can be and is pleased with us who believe in Jesus His Son. Upon the announcing the birth of Jesus the angels said this;

Glory to God in the highest, And peace on earth among men 'with whom He is pleased' Luke 2:14

Are you not sure if God is pleased with you?

God is pleased when you accept Jesus as your savior.

God is pleased when you got baptised.

God is pleased to give you the holy spirit.

God is pleased that you love Him.

God is pleased to give grace to you even though you could not earn it.

God is pleased When you talk to Him.

God is pleased when you worship Him.

God is pleased when you show His love towards people.

God is please when you speak about His Love to other people.

God is pleased when you give Him glory.

I could go on and on, But you see that God is pleased. If you add all these and more things together You could easily say that God is, **well pleased**, with us. It is all a matter of prospective. You can believe that you will never be worthy, or you can believe that Jesus has made you worthy.

You can believe that God will never accept you, unless you do this and that. Beat yourself down and grovel in sackcloth and ashes. Or you can stand up with Jesus because you have been given the righteousness of God. He placed it inside you through faith. God says that we can come into His presence with boldness.

You cannot teach children these things unless you know and believe them yourselves. How can you teach children to come to the throne of grace with confidence, if you are not sure about this for yourself. We know that we are forgiven yet come to God in fear of what He may think of us. This does not make sense. God does not have the attitude that He is not going to listen to you, because you got angry with your spouse an hour ago and said some horrible things.

There is a chapter in the old testament that talks about the benefits of what Jesus did when He died on the cross. It is in Isaiah. These are the promises of God to all who are born again into the new life in Jesus Christ. The whole chapter is about Gods promises to us, it is a good read, and we should make the promises personal to ourselves. But I just wish to highlight one small part of them to you, believer in Jesus Christ.

So I have sworn that I will not be angry with you, nor will I rebuke you Isaiah 54:10

We have to begin to understand who we are in Christ Jesus, Then we can teach our children who they are in Christ Jesus. I have to tell you that words are the most powerful weapons that we have to build each other up, in the Lord. **Death and life are in the power of the tongue.** We are what we speak. What we say, what comes out of our mouths in speech affects us, as well as those we speak to. It can cause sickness to come upon us, and other curses too. This is what Jesus said:

After Jesus called the crowd to Him, He said, "Hear and understand. It is not what enters into the mouth that defiles a man, but what proceeds from out of the mouth, this defiles a man." Matthew 15:10-11

Words are seeds that are planted within our hearts. All words, both good and bad. If we allow bad seeds to be planted, then our hearts will become corrupted and it will come out in the words we say. And become a curse to those who hear. Or ourselves. On the other hand if we plant seeds of the truth of the word of God in our hearts, they will grow and our hearts will be purified, and the fruit of goodness and truth will come forth from our mouths. Our words will become a blessing to those who hear.

Every word is a seed. Every word you hear, from people in person, everything you listen to on television or radio; Every song you listen to, every sermon you hear. Every word you say, because it comes out of your mouth, back into your ears and into your heart. Then it comes out again through your mouth, with more conviction than before. It does not matter if it is good or bad, it always works the same way.

It is a good thing to read the word of God out loud for this very reason. As Christians we should be using this principle to strengthen our faith, and the faith of others around us, and that includes children.

This is what psychology is all about, building positive mental attitudes. This has to start with our children from the day they are born. You have to have a positive mental attitude, you pass it on to your children, all attitudes are infectious.

Think about it, it is true. Yes you can break out of the cycle, but why infect children with the wrong attitude in the first place? Simple things like, putting a plaster/band-aid onto a cut or graze will make it better. No it will not, it will to stop any further infection, but do not lie. The body actually heals itself, makes itself better.

I have heard the word 'kidology' used so many times even used it myself in the past. It is just lying to get a child to do, or be the way you want. Why do people use tricks in their words to achieve what they want. It is psychology. The psychology of the Christian should be the truth of the word of God. You have to trust what god's word says. This is faith.

Without faith it is impossible to please God. Hebrews 11.

We should be teaching children to trust God's word. To have faith in what God's word says about them. As a Christian you are a new creation, old things have passed away and everything has become new. As children, growing, we learn to obey our sinful nature, our unrenewed spirit.

We learn to sin from our spirit, because it is our sinful nature. It is infected by the corruption of Satan from the beginning when he deceived Eve into eating of the fruit, from the tree of knowledge. When we are born again, we get a new spirit. From God, that is sealed with the Holy Spirit. This is what it means when the word of God says, "All things have become new."

God sees you in respect of your new spirit. A spirit that is as pure as Jesus' Spirit. A spirit that is the way it was before Adam and Eve sinned. God Has done this, so you can meet with Him every day. Just like he used to with Adam and Eve in the Garden of Eden. This is what God wants, He does not wish for any of us to be hiding, because we think we are naked!

God created Adam and Eve naked. He did not give them any clothes to wear, and God walked with them and had fellowship with them every day. It was not a problem for God. It became a problem for Adam and Eve, in their minds. They became psychologically aware of their nakedness. So to protect them from their own conscience, God made them some clothes out of animal skins. Way back then, in the Garden of Eden, psychology began.

That's when deception began. Satan did not ask a straight question of Eve, He used deception that is what 'kidology' is. It comes from the devil. You may argue this point. That is like saying a little white lie does not count! It is still a lie, no matter how big it is.

We should only tell the truth. To lie to a child, is to teach that child to lie. it to teach them that it is OK to lie. That is not the way we want to raise our children. when it is put plainly like this it is obvious. Everything we say has consequences. Everything we do has consequences.

That is what the Old Testament law was about, consequences and blessings for obeying, and also consequences and curses for disobedience. We teach children to live under the way of law, rather the way of grace. This is the punishment for disobeying. That is it, what about the blessings for obedience. We do not teach this. What about telling your children that you forgive them, when they have done something wrong?

From experience, it is more like tell them off, and let them stew in their guiltiness for a while. But do you ever tell them that you forgive them. Well it does happen I know, but for most the parents stay angry at the child for much longer than they ought to. I would go as far as saying that you should not even get angry.

For the anger of man does not achieve the righteousness of God. James 1:20

Getting angry at children, at anybody is not good, for them or you. This type of anger can eat away at your own self esteem. Can cause you distress and sickness as much as it can cause for the person you are angry at. Most of the time anger is used as a retaliation, towards someone who you think has done you wrong.

The word of God says it is OK to get angry, but not to let your anger cause you to sin. When you let your anger cause you to sin, then you open yourself up to the devil coming at you with sicknesses, and anything else he can use against you.

When does your anger cause you to sin? Simple, when it is directed at another person. You can be angry at what the devil is doing through somebody, but do not be angry with the person. This is truth that we should be teaching children. Trouble is a lot of adult Christians do not understand these things. So the teaching of children becomes a nonevent. This is because if you cannot manage your own emotions, then you cannot teach others to manage theirs.

Managing Emotions

Through our lives we go through many emotional changes. Even as we go through each day. We can be, happy, sad, excited, downbeat, lonely, at peace, angry, all in one day. So how do we get to a position where we become stable in our emotions? Is it at all possible to become stable emotionally?

What I mean by this is that we get to a point where we see that even the biggest upset in our lives, does not tip us over the edge emotionally. A place where we can reason things and be at peace no matter what. That is not to say that we never get shaken, but no matter how hard the shaking is we remain firmly rooted in the stability of our emotions. This can only come through a stability of a good relationship with God, through Jesus.

Yes, your emotions can become stable. They are a part of who you are. They do not have to knock you sideways, every time something happens that shakes you. Emotions are supposed to be good for us, but through sin we have allowed some of them to become bad. Most of these come through fear. Even to the point that we are supposed to have a fear of God.

I am talking about a negative fear, that God is always ready to punish us if we put a foot wrong. As I have already pointed out, that God says that He will not be angry with us or rebuke us. It is not God that will condemn us, but our own hearts. We can allow our hearts to condemn us. This is what It says in God's word.

Beloved, if our heart does not condemn us, we have confidence before God; 1 John 3:21

All we have to do to have this confidence is to,

believe in the name of His Son, Jesus Christ, and love one another as He commanded. 1 John 3:23

What the word of God says about fearing God has more to do with honor and respect for God, than being afraid of His judgment, or potential anger towards us. This is a fear of the devil; he has created it. It is not the truth; it is a lie. Because we have this wrong attitude about God and His anger, we use the same principles on our children.

We consider that we have a right to get angry with them for something they do wrong. That is not how God treats us. So we should not treat others like this either. Especially children, who are made in the image of God just as we are. So what does the word of God say about managing our emotions?

Actually an enormous amount. Most of it is about what God will do to help and protect us. So many in the psalms, to choose from. Read and apply them to yourself. I will highlight just a couple. **Psalm 23** is a great testimony to the protection of God. We should have no fear.

Even though I walk through the valley of the shadow of death, I *will* fear no evil, for Thou art with me. Psalm 23:4

The steps of a man are established by the Lord; And He delights in his way. When he falls he shall not be hurled headlong; Because the Lord is the One who holds his hand. Psalm 37:23

God is our refuge and strength, a very present help in trouble therefore we will not fear. Psalm 46:1-2

There are many verses like these in just the psalms. That is under the old covenant. Since Jesus we are told that there is therefore now No condemnation for us in Christ Jesus. It is a matter of knowing who we are in Jesus Christ. Know what the word of God says about us. Jesus said, "I will never leave you, nor forsake you."

The book of Romans is a great place to see who we are, and what God has done for us. Here is just a couple of examples.

Therefore, having been justified by faith, we have peace with God through our Lord Jesus Christ Romans 5:1

Nothing shall be able to separate us from the love of God, which is in Christ Jesus our Lord. Romans 8:39

Jesus said that we should not worry, but seek first the Kingdom of God. Do you know that if we seek firstly the kingdom of God, we would not even be aware of any negative emotions. I remember the words to a famous hymn, 'and the things of this world will grow strangely dim, in the light of His glory and grace.' To manage our emotions we should be looking to God.

If we are truly seeking God, there would be only the fruit of the Spirit rising up from within us. These are the positive emotions that God has placed within us, for not only our benefit, but for the benefit of all those who are a part of our lives. No matter how fleeting the encounter is.

Ephesians 1 says that God has blessed us with every Spiritual blessing, in heavenly places. What this means, is that every Spiritual blessing that is in heavenly places we have. It is not still in the heavenly places; we are blessed with it here on earth.

If it was still in the heavenly places, we have not been blessed with it yet. It is still waiting for us at some future date. No God Has already blessed us. I hope you get what I am saying. That there is no reason for having negative emotions, if you know what the word of God says about you.

We have received the Spirit who is from God, that we might know the things freely given to us by God. 1 Corinthians 2:12

You have the mind of Christ. 1 Corinthians 2:16

I could go on and on with the promises of God, that should negate any negative emotions. They are there written down for us all to see, in God's word. The biggest problem is that we do not put a priority on reading God's word. Receiving and applying what it says to our own lives, We tend to stick a **BUT!** in the way If you do not read it, the chances are you will never hear God speak to you.

Everything that we need to live a victorious life with positive emotions is right there in our bibles. It is the bread of life. We cannot live without it, you think you can, maybe for a little while, but your Spiritual life will die. Why do our young children not have a spiritual life, Because we do not make the word of God an essential part of everyday life for them, as well as for ourselves. If we did, they would know and experience all the blessings and positive emotions, that God has given freely to us all who believe in Jesus.

Thou wilt keep him in prefect peace, whose mind is stayed on thee: because he trusteth thee.

Isaiah 26:3 KJV

The bible is just so full of positive affirmations about who we are, and how we should view ourselves. And the promises of God towards us as His children, Fellow heirs with Christ, to all that God has prepared for those who love Him. If we trusted the word of God there would not be any room for negative emotions. There should be no reason for feeling down, depressed, angry at people, or the world.

My mum used to remind us as children, that there is always someone worse off than you. We have got a house to live in; we have got food to eat; I can grow food and I do; I have got a car to drive; I have a fit and healthy body, even at sixty years old.

There is always something to thank, and give praise to the Lord for. The trees, the birds, The moon and stars. This creation is so marvelous, and perfectly formed. Everything works together just right. The moon causes the ocean tides to ebb and flow, so that all over the world we have high tides and low tides, for our benefit.

We have day and night, warmth of the sun. Seasons so that we can grow food, and give the earth time to rest before we plant again. On and on there is so much out there to praise God for. Yet so many of us are only inward looking. What we can do to improve our lot in life. When the word says:

Delight yourself in the Lord, and He will give you the desires of your heart. Psalm 37:4

This is the cure for probably all emotional illnesses. Delight yourself in the Lord. Fill yourself with His word, Put on the Lord Jesus Christ, every day. You can do it and you can show your children how to do it. If you are not sure, you can learn. Teach yourself and your children at the same time. This is not something where you have to become perfect first. It is called growing together. Give thanks to God every day, in all things. You will then have peace.

But in everything by prayer and supplication, with <u>thanksgiving</u> let your requests be made known to God. And the peace of God that surpasses all comprehension, will guard your hearts and your minds in Christ Jesus. Philippians 4:6-7

Give thanks to God. Praise Him for all you are, and all He has made you to be. If you cannot think of anything to praise God for. You are probably dead.

There are many more good, and positive things happening in the world, than there are bad negative things. If you do not have Jesus in your life, I could maybe understand some negative emotions. If we are born again and Spirit filled there is absolutely not any reason to be depressed, anxious, or fearful in any way. I do know that not everyone can see it this way, but why not?

We can open the door to these things anxiety and depression...... and let them come and dominate our lives. We are supposed to let the Holy Spirit come and comfort us, So we can let the LOVE of God dominate our lives. So if you are clothed with depression or any kind of fear, take it off and put on the Lord Jesus. If you dwell on the negative, you will feel negative, become negative, live negative be negative. If you dwell on the good and positive, you will feel positive, become positive, live positive, be positive. I know that this is why Paul wrote the following verse, following on from the above verse. It is all about what you think about.

Finally, brethren, whatever is true, whatever is honorable, whatever is right, Whatever is pure, whatever is lovely, whatever is of good repute, if there is any excellence, and if anything worthy of praise, dwell on these things. The thing you have learned and received in me, practice these thing, and the peace of God will be with you.
Philippians 4:8-9

Peace is everything in Jesus. It is the emotion that can rule all emotions. You can feel at peace with something, doing something, going somewhere. If you do not have peace with something you should question if that thing is right. That is one way the Holy Spirit leads us. You cannot have peace if you do not love, We need both, the Love of God, that will bring peace. God extended peace and good will to all men, that's what the angels said to the shepherds. So many times in the writings of the epistles, peace is extended as a blessing upon the people of God's church. Jesus said this:

My peace I give to you; not as the world gives do I give to you. Do not let your heart be troubled, nor let it be fearful John 14:27

There it is again, we have peace because Jesus gave it to us, 'Do Not Let Your Heart Be Troubled.' This is a command. You have a choice to not let your heart be troubled. Or let your heart be troubled. To be fearful, or not fearful. What do want to choose? What will be best for your children? We all want the best for our children, I know, that is why we have to teach them the right things in the right way.

There are scriptures to fit every situation that you or your children might find yourselves in. Scripture that will help you, show you the way, give you understanding.

No matter what you need. Jesus said, "Cast your burdens upon Him," and He means it. Give them to Him you do not have to carry them. They should not be bothering you, to take your mind away from the truth of God's word.

Freedom

That is how the enemy operates. He will get you focusing on something that distracts you from the truth, from what you know from Gods word. You know how it is, you get up in the morning and you have to deal with some calamity, with a child. Then it makes you run a bit late. That puts everything behind, So what happens? You skip your devotional time with God to try to make some time back.

That's it he did it, the devil distracted you from the word. Now all day you may, have problems, not because you missed devotions, but you allowed the devil, to distract you. You opened the door for him to cause hindrances all day. It is not because he was able to distract you, it is because you feel like somehow you have not fulfilled a daily requirement. Your religious duty.

It does not matter whether it is the devil, or just your own conscience, you let the thing ruin your whole day. When you could have prayed while doing something else, like driving to work. Or even just to stop for a few seconds and say,

"Lord help me through this day."

Sometimes we are just too hard on ourselves. There have been some men mighty of God, who spent less than thirty minutes a day, both praying and studying the bible who God used to create big revivals, men who god used to heal many people. These men were just men of faith.

They believed what they read in the bible. They believed, and accepted it as true. Then they operated in faith believing that God would use them to do healings and miracles. Our children if they are taught that The Word is Truth, and see us adults walking in the power of the truth, then they will know it is true. Jesus said:

If you abide in My word, then you are truly disciples of mine; and you shall know the truth, and the truth shall set you free. John 8:31-32

You will be set free from the bondage of the wisdom of the world. This is quite hard To accomplish when we have grown up under the worlds way of thinking, and lived according to the worlds doctrines of how we should think, speak, and act. It is bondage.

Are you not sure of this statement? I know that it is bondage, and so many of you know that it is bondage, simply by this. When you opened your heart to the Lord and accepted Him as your Savior, there was what seemed like a release. You felt something lift from you, like an oppression. You felt set free.

That is what the bible says, we have been set free from the bondage of the law. The law of sin and death no longer has dominion over us. That means that the devil no longer has dominion over us. We are free from his bondage, but many of us do not understand or realise this.

Even in some churches they preach and teach, that obeying the law will, help you get to heaven, this is not true. This is old testament thinking. Old covenant doctrine, deception of the truth. Doctrine of the devil.

The devil would love to have everyone trying to live according to the law.

The truth is this, when we are born again our old nature is replaced with a new nature. Our old spirit is replaced with the new spirit, from God. The Holy Spirit will not let anything corrupt our new spirit. If we then are allowing the Holy Spirit lead and guide us. Then it will be impossible for us to violate the law, and have it corrupt our new spirit/nature.

So we naturally obey the law without trying. You actually have to think about sinning before you can sin. This helps us to resist and stay free. You actually recognise when sinful thoughts come into your head, and you can deal with them before they can be of any corruptible influence on your soul.

We are destroying speculations, and every lofty thing raised up against the knowledge of God, we are taking every thought captive to the obedience of Christ. 2 Corinthians10:5

How do we do this? By renewing our mind through reading the word of God, and allowing ourselves to be open to being led by the Spirit. This is the freedom that we have if we choose, in Christ. The freedom to be free of the consciousness of sin. To live a life free of any condemnation. This is available to us through Jesus, it is available to everyone who will believe.

It does not matter how old you are, Jesus has set us free. We can and should be teaching this freedom to children. It is important for them as much as it is for us adults. Every man woman and child needs to know, how to renew their mind, and how to be led by the Spirit.

For all who are being led by the Spirit of God, are the sons of God Romans 8:14

But if you are led by the Spirit you are not under the Law. Galatians 5:18

Freedom, we are free. You me and all who have come to know God. If you know Him you will be led by His Spirit. Everyone needs to know our heavenly Father. Everyone means everyone. You do not have the right to withhold the knowledge of God from anyone.

I am speaking to myself here too. As I recall from my past, the feeling that I should say something to someone, and have not, through some fear. It was the Spirit leading me where I was afraid to go. Then I did not understand, or realise the freedom that I had been granted from God.

So, I had fears. Fears of rejection, thinking about it I have to ask why? Because I would not be the one being rejected, they would have been rejecting God and His word. Another fear would have been fear of what the person would think of me. I knew the scripture, but did not have it planted solidly in my heart, that says:

The Lord is my rock and my salvation, My stronghold, I will not be shaken. Psalm 62:6

Strength

Knowledge is strength, We are told to be strong in the Lord. How can we be strong in the Lord if we do not know what His word says? How can we know God without knowing His word? **In the beginning was the Word.... and the word was God.** You cannot be strong and be led by the Spirit, without the knowledge of the word of God.

God lives in His word. It is active, it is always working to establish God's kingdom. The Armor of God is all about the word; the word of God to protect you, to protect your mind. It is knowing God's word that is knowing God. If you hear, or read something that does not line up with the word of God, then it is not truth. You can only trust the truth. By trusting the truth of God's word, is the only way to be strong in the Lord and the strength of His might.

Finally, be strong in the Lord and the strength of His might. Put on the full armor of God, so that you may be able to stand firm against the schemes of the devil. Ephesians 6:10-11

The devil uses psychology all the time, he attacks us though our minds. He gets us to question what we know is right, usually by suggesting an alternative. A way that seems right to a man. Not everything that seems right is right. That is why we need to be led by the Spirit, reminding us of the truth of the Word of God. That is the Holy Spirits job, to lead us into all the truth. To tell us what is right and wrong, to remind us of God's word. That is the strength of the Lord working in and through our lives.

The devil does not care who he uses, he just wants to disrupt our faith. He will use spouse, friend, relative, even your children. So it follows that if you can get your children to walk by and be led by the Spirit, you would have a more peaceful life. Now I know that this is not a reason for getting children to be led by the Spirit, but it will be the fruit of it. Yes, we all want the best for our children, but it has to be the best as God see's it not us with a worldly sense of values. We have to use God's values.

So again in this as with all other things in life, we should seek first the Kingdom of God. Not only that, we should get to a place where seeking God over things becomes a natural every minute of the day experience. You will probably say that this is not reasonable. Why not? I know that I am not the only one, but I am always praying, there is always something to pray about, even just to say, "Thanks Lord."

Rejoice always; pray without ceasing; in everything give thanks; for this is God's will for you in Christ Jesus. Do not quench the Spirit.
1 Thessalonians 5:16-19

It is all about a fellowship, a relationship with God. When you know God and can talk to Him about everything, that is strength. You have peace, in your mind and in your heart. That is strength. There are four things in the above verses.

1 Rejoice always.

I remember back in the 1980's some of us had the habit of saying, "Praise the Lord anyway." It is like no matter what was happening you just have to praise the Lord. Just like Paul and Silas in prison, praising the Lord at midnight. Then all the chains fell off and all the prison doors opened. The whole prison was caught up with the Spirit of praise that no one made a run for it.

2 Pray without ceasing,

I have already covered this a little. But we should be praying about every situation, it is a continual communion with God. Being so in tune with the Spirit of God that it talks to you as you go about your daily life. As I said it is a relationship, but like no other you will ever have. As the Spirit teaches, guides and even tells you what is going to happen. This does not happen overnight, it needs to be cultivated, just like any relationship.

3 Give thanks in everything.

Not for everything, but in everything. There is a difference. Not everything is from God, but the devil tries to bring things into our lives that we do not need, we do not need to cultivate. These are things to give thanks that God is with us as we go through whatever it is. That He has given us authority over everything that the devil tries to bring us into. Give thanks that we have the authority to speak against the thing and rebuke it.

4 Do not quench the Spirit.

It is a fact that so many of us can quench the Spirit and what he wants to work in and through us. That is why God says to not quench the Spirit. We quench the Spirit by doing things in our own strength, not relying upon the Spirit to lead us. Not clothing ourselves with our new self, will give the devil opportunity to deceive us and lead us astray. If we are led by the Spirit, we will be strong enough to stand against the whiles of the devil. That is what the armor of God is all about. Putting on the new self so that you can protect your mind.

And that you be renewed it the spirit of your mind, and put on the new self, which in the likeness of God has been created in righteousness and holiness of the truth. Ephesians 4:23-24

Change of psychology

Why a chapter on psychology in a Christian book? Psychology is the science of the mind. God speaks to us about our minds, all through His word. Be transformed by the renewing of your mind. We have to use the mind of Christ which we have through the Holy Spirit.

It is our thoughts that will corrupt us, if we allow. That is what happened before. Thoughts become desires then desires rule over our hearts. God sees the thoughts and intentions of our hearts. Way back when God decided to flood the earth and destroy everything, He had looked and said this:

Then the Lord saw that the wickedness of man was great on the earth, and that every intent of the thoughts of his heart was only evil continually Genesis 6:5

God made a promise never to destroy creation again with a flood. It is a promise, an unconditional covenant. The only condition in the new covenant is that we accept Jesus as Savior. That is the point where our psychology begins to change, we become a new creation. We begin to see things differently, and so begin to think differently. We begin to grow in faith, a gift from God. Faith is a decision of the mind.

The Holy Spirit begins to teach us. The thoughts and intentions of our hearts begin to change. We are happy to fill our minds with the things of God. This in turn, fills our thoughts and hearts with new and holy desires. Seeking the kingdom of God, rather our own selfish desires.

A change of psychology begins. We should nurture this every day. We can help the Spirit to help us. We do this by praying, and reading God's word, seeking answers. When you think that You know it all, it is because you have stopped seeking. This is all revelation to me as I write. I am teaching myself through the words I write and read back to myself.

There have been periods in my life that I stopped seeking, and so stopped receiving words from the Lord. Now as I type the words are just coming into my mind, a steady stream of revelation. Tuned into the Holy Spirit, receiving that which belongs to Jesus, the Spirit is giving to me. Teaching me. That is what the Spirit does.

My thoughts and desires before beginning this book was to become a driving instructor. Thinking that it will provide me with a good ongoing income way after my retirement age. Thinking that it was me who had to cause my provision, rather relying upon Jehovah Jireh, to be my provider.

This was MY thinking, the psychology of the world for providing for myself and family. Also I don't see that at the age of Sixty-seven, I will be too old to be a productive person, It is a time of life, yes to look at new possibilities for the future. Not a time to shut down and become a tired, do nothing vegetable.

That is the world's way of thinking, the worlds psychology, that says that at certain age you are no longer able to function efficiently as part of the ever changing workplace and population. I was even working out how much I could save, for how many years, and how it would be invested to provide extra when I did have to give up work. This is worldly thinking, the psychology of the world.

For My thoughts are not your thoughts, neither are your ways My ways, declares the Lord. For as the heavens are higher than the earth, so are My ways higher than your ways, and My thoughts than your thoughts. Isaiah 55:8-9

So even after over forty years of being a Christian I struggled between the psychology of the world, and the reasoning guidance, psychology of the Christian faith. The reason for this is I know that I have still remnants of the worlds way of thinking going on in my mind. I grew up following the worlds psychologies for living. The worlds reasons for doing things, the worlds ways of achieving, following the direction of the spirit of the world.

I learned this from day that I was born for nearly twenty years. Twenty years of spirit of the worlds indoctrination. Lies and misleading. Twenty years of wrong teaching. Twenty years of wrong psychology.

You may ask, "what makes you any different to the rest of us?" good question, the answer is absolutely nothing. That is the very point that I am trying to make. If we were all filled with teaching and leading of the Holy Spirit from birth, we would all have grown up differently. Yes, we still would have had to come to a point that we had to decide to accept Jesus as our Savior.

I know that this would have come to a point at a much earlier age, as children. Then there would be so much less of the worlds psychology to counteract. Put it another way, Much less of the worlds teaching and indoctrination to change in our minds. We would have had a better idea of the plans that God has for our lives. We would be able to see things more clearly from God's point of view, instead of the world's viewpoint.

Chapter 9: Discipline

Discipline is a touchy topic that is very, or can be very tricky when talking to others about how to train their children. Every body seems to have their own point of view, and ideas of how to raise their children. 'And don't anybody dare tell me how to do it! Or that, 'I am doing it wrong!' Some say that there is no right or wrong way, because every child is different, and you have to adapt to the child.

Much of this is down to projected political correctness and personal experience. It is not that any of these are wrong, it is about as the bible says, to raise a child in the way he should go. The things that we teach children and ideas that we give them; the way that we treat them, is the way they grow up thinking that that is the way things should be done. Yes every child is different, unique. There will not be another who will respond the way they do, to the way that you say, or do things.

There is a difference between discipline and chastisement. The trouble is now, that everything comes under the title of discipline. Such as disciplinary hearings, to dish out or decide what kind of punishment is to be dished out. As with much of Christian teaching the lines have become blurred between the two different things. In the Old testament God gave the law, this for training, showing how people ought to be.

Discipline!

On the other hand there also came with the law, consequences for breaking the law. This is punishment, Chastisement. Yes, chastisement can be used as part of discipline to train a person not to do the wrong thing again.

This is not a book about raising children but more of study how to treat children as fellow heirs to the Kingdom of God. With that in mind let's look at what discipline is. If you are disciplined, you are trained in how to behave, act, or work in a particular way. You can be disciplined to do things in a bad way or a good way. There is bad and good discipline. Most of the time bad discipline is called undisciplined. Which is actually not really true. Undisciplined means to not be trained.

In sports for instance, some people are disciplined to do everything by the rules. Then there are some who have trained themselves in how to cheat without getting caught. Both are disciplined in their respective arts. Both have trained much to be good at the things that they do, one in doing things right, and the other one in cheating.

In sports there are there are many different disciplines. Some are called disciplines for the reason that there are, within one sport different disciplines. Take athletics for instance. Many different sports within one umbrella name. So you either train for the high jump or throwing the javelin. When you get good you are called disciplined in that area of training.

You discipline yourself to become good at something. Sometimes you get a trainer who helps you to become more disciplined. Someone to set out what needs to be done to help you get better and move up to the next level of competency. Someone who gets to know your strengths, and weaknesses and can help you to become stronger all round.

The point that I am making is that discipline is training. When it says in the bible, 'train a child up in the way that it should go,' it is just that, training, teaching. This is done as much by example as it is by instruction. Children will do as you do. Even if you say something different they will see that, what you do is the way to do. Until they get trained to do in a better way. It is kind of like when you get a job, you get trained to do that job in a particular way. The biggest part of the training is being physically shown what to do and how to do it.

Also part of that training is being told and shown what to do if something goes wrong. Then through experience you learn how to deal with thing without having to keep calling for help, to sort a problem out. This is when you get disciplined at the work you are doing.

Discipline verses chastisement

On the other hand, chastisement is something different. Too many people confuse chastisement with discipline. It is true that chastisement can be used to install discipline, but it is not really training. This is because the use of chastisement has become more of just punishment rather than a tool to be used to train. It is used more often to beat someone down rather than to help build them up. Mostly it is more to do with forcing your will upon someone else. Making them to become what you want them to be. Forcing their will to become the same as yours.

This is not the way that God is. He has never been this way. He created man with a free will, with the choice to do right or wrong. The choice to choose life or death. He will not violate your will with His. God wants us to choose to follow His will. He wants to have a relationship with us, He wants for us to fellowship with Him. God is love and will not ever beat us down until we submit to Him. That is not God's personality.

That is why we have God's word. It is our training manual; we can choose to follow it or choose not to. There is a benefit to following Gods word, and also consequences for not. It is the same for every area of our lives. The benefits for doing things right is always greater than if we cut corners.

The problem that we have as humans, is that we follow after the ways in which we are raised or trained. Whatever that regime might be, we carry it forward. We tend to use the same methods on our children that were used on us. It does not matter whether they were right, or wrong, good or bad.

It is the same in a job. Let's say you start working at a new company, doing something that you have never done before. You know little or nothing about how to do the work. Someone comes along to train you how to do it. They teach you the wrong things, the wrong way to do the work. You do not know it is wrong, you just do as you are told. As far as you know What you were told is the right way to do the work.

We are creatures of habit. How many times do we see the stories of people who are caught in some wrongdoing, and their story seems to be a continuation of the life that they grew up in. For instance, people convicted of sexual crimes, turn out to have been victims of sex crime when they were children. People convicted of brutal abuse of their partner grew up with that same thing happening around them. It is the influence of the prince of the power of the air.

That is the influence behind the environment in which these people grew up. We pass on what we know, good or bad. This should not be, to some extent we cannot help it. Our lives have been under the influence of the prince of the power of the air. we should only pass on that which is good. Something that we cannot do until we work on the renewing of the mind, according to the word of God.

And you were dead in your trespasses and sins, in which you formally walked according to the course of this world, according to the prince of the power of the air, of the spirit that is now working in the sons of disobedience. Ephesians 2:1-2

As Christians we should be doing things in a better way as far as raising our children. Setting better examples. Not be the same as our unsaved neighbours. Chastisement is important, but chastisement does not mean beating into submission. There may be times when a smack may be necessary, there are alternative methods of punishments that can be used. Beating a child into submission is not right.

As I said, discipline is all about training, not about forcing. It is about teaching and guiding and leading, into truth through love. You see, if God cannot make you love Him, make you obey Him. If God cannot force you to follow Him and do His will. Why Do we think that we can treat children this way, to force them into submission. Forcing someone, anyone to do something, or be something against their will, can open a door to allow a spirit or rebellion access into that person.

If you show them love train them in a spirit of love, they will love and submit to your authority. It will be their choice. That is how God works. He Loved the world so much that He gave His Son Jesus, to show us and help us have a relationship with His Father. God works through love, not through violence. God calls us to Himself, He does not herd us with a whip, to go where He wants. Violence so much of the time creates rebellion.

There is an old saying that is much used in the military, it goes like this. 'A volunteer is worth twenty pressed men.' This is not always true, but someone who is willing is twenty times happier to comply than someone who is forced to comply. Sometimes we think that our children _have_ to do and be what we say, simply because we are the adults, and the parents. But what if that child came to you with some wisdom from God. You know it was from God. Are you humble enough to be told by your child the way you should be, or go, or what you should do.

There is a story in the bible about this I want you to look at. But a lot of people would spend a lot of time questioning the things, or even say I am not going to be told by a child what to do. We have an attitude that we always know what is best for a child, not that a child could teach us anything. The thing is, can God teach us anything through a child? We are told to have child-like faith.

The biblical story is to do with Samuel, I am sure that most people have heard of it. Samuel was just a young boy. While he was laying down, maybe sleeping he heard the voice of God, calling his name. Samuel did not understand that I was God, so he went to the High Priest, thinking it was Eli calling. After this happened three times, Eli realised that it was God who was calling Samuel. Eli told Samuel that if God calls him again, he should just say,

"Speak Lord your servant is listening." Samuel 3:9

God spoke to Samuel and gave him his first prophesy, about the judgement upon Eli's house because of a curse that Eli's sons had brought upon themselves. That Eli had failed to rebuke his sons. Now Eli was like a father figure to Samuel, it says that Samuel was afraid to tell Eli what God had said. But Eli was wise, and humble enough to listen to what God had to say through Samuel. Because whatever it was, it was a message from God.

I was thinking about this whole thing. It shows me that even though Eli was old and wise, he knew that God was God. He knew that if God wanted to use a little boy to speak God's word he should be humble enough to listen. It is still the word of God, no matter who's mouth it comes from. This was the discipline of Eli to listen and accept whatever God said.

The judgement was the punishment for not previously acting according to God's will and rebuking his sons. The point is this, we need to be aware that God can use our children to speak to us, and to teach us. Are we disciplined enough to understand this truth.

Chastisement includes rebuking and punishment. Rebuking is not cursing. It is, stopping someone from doing wrong telling them to get right, to repent. To turn from wrong to right. They may need stern words; it may become a big argument. But they have to be told. This is also a form of disciplining. Rebuking gives a person the opportunity to repent, and change, before you get to the punishment stage.

I remember that when I was a boy; the times that I did something wrong; I was rebuked and was told this, many times, I have to wait for my punishment. You know the old saying, "Wait until your dad gets home." When dad got home it was told what I had done, then dad would deal out the punishment. Whether I had repented or not!

It did not matter if any of us were repentant, or even said sorry for what we had done wrong. Our punishment was on its way, when dad got home. We had to be punished yes we probably deserved the punishment. But that is not Discipline. There was discipline in between chastisement, and the punishment. Plenty of time to consider the results of our actions. Time to evaluate how perhaps next time not to get caught. This is because we were not taught the Truth, the Way, or the Life. We were not disciplined.

God's way, under the new covenant.

We all know and have heard that God is love. We have also heard other things, like 'Spare the rod, spoil the child.' maybe your heard something like this, 'If I did not love you I would not beat you.' Is that the way that God is? Does God expect us to behave in this way? No! and No! If God gave us a smack on the head every time we said, did or thought something wrong, we would end up being battered and bruised.

God loved the world so much, that He did not destroy it and everyone on the face of the earth, He sent His only Son Jesus. Why So that through Jesus we would be able to know God the Father. That is what God wants, that is his love, that through Jesus all the sin of the world is forgiven. We did not deserve it, but He did it anyway. So that we can have a relationship with and know God. That is what Jesus said I came that you may know the Father. Many times in different ways.

For God so loved the world that He gave His only begotten Son, that whoever believes in Him, shall not Perish, but Have eternal life. John 3:16

This is eternal life, that they may know You, the only true God, and Jesus Christ whom You have

sent......... and I have made Your name known to them, and will make it known, so that the love with which You loved Me may be in them, and I in them. John 17:3, 26

God is not going to judge us or chastise us or rebuke us. It is a promise of God, written down in Isaiah 54. It is God's word. Do you believe God's word. God will never be angry with us. He has set us free from the law of sin and death. He has forgiven us, forever. He does not even remember our sins. He does not want to remember them. Yet we so often like to remind Him. Why? Maybe because we like to remember the things that people have done against us and bring it up every-time it becomes convenient. Because we do this, we sort of think that God is the same.

So we come to Him in fear and trembling, hoping He will not remind us of that thing we did last week or month. We are the ones who remember, and remind Him, then we think it is God's conviction. It is not, it is our own hearts. The devil then comes in to make us feel so unworthy. The devil loves it when we give him something to chew on. We make it easy for him, we open doors and windows to him that have been shut. They were shut when you accepted Jesus as Saviour.

As far as the east is from the west, so far has He removed our transgressions from us. Psalm 103:12

This is something that we forget too easily. We forget what God has done, and what His character is like. We remember the awesome vengeful God from the old testament, who punished His chosen people, for disobedience. We forget that God also blessed His people, all the time. He did not remove His blessing from the children of Israel. For forty years in the wilderness he fed and gave them water. Their clothes and shoes never wore out. He fought battles for them, and defeated enemies.

Moses actually told god to repent at One time from a decision He had made to destroy the people. God said of His people to Balaam that he is not allowed to curse the people because they are blessed.

So under the old covenant, God was a God of love and reason. God is always ready to forgive. He always has been this way. Under the new covenant, God has bound Himself by His word. He loves us his people and He wants for us to love others in the same way that He loves us, especially our brothers and sisters in Christ. It does not matter how old, or young they are. It does not matter if the children belong to someone else, or our own. They belong to God just as you and I do. As we have seen earlier in this book, it seems that God places a high value upon our children who believe in Him. We should have a great respect of that attitude of God.

God desires for us to raise our children to know God, just as Jesus came so that we may know God. He is our Father; He is also your children's Father. Yet we often train our children up under judgement and condemnation, rather than train them up in love. So as you can see, there is something wrong. It has to be the way that we as adults, think about the way that is right to treat children.

Jesus said, "let the children come. Do not hinder the children." Judgement and condemnation is creating a stumbling block to children. We as fathers especially should be showing to our children the grace of God. We should be a reflection to our children, of how God our Father treats us. This is what the word of God says to fathers, about treatment of their children.

Fathers do not exasperate your children, that they may not lose heart. Colossians 3:21

The word exasperate here means do not anger your children, or provoke them to anger. To me that means that fathers should not be angry towards children. You can be angry at what has been done, but not angry at them. When My children were children, and if I got angry with them, I always waited until my anger had died down before I went to talk to them about the thing.

I knew that in anger it is easy to lose control. Yes I would have to raise my voice and send them to their room. But I would never talk to them about what they had done while I was angry. It is almost impossible to be reasonable, or use reason, when anger burns within you. Think about that for a while, can you be reasonable, have reasonable thoughts while angry?

Then there are the results of dealing with your child through your anger. Anger is infectious, it causes another to become angry in defense or defiance. It causes resentment, and bitterness. Which in turn can go on to cause all sorts of mental problems. I have seen first-hand how bitterness can work in, and through someone. Bitterness blocks out reason and reasonable thought. If we cannot talk to someone with sound reasoning, in a reasonable manner, then we should keep quiet.

Let no unwholesome word proceed from your mouth, but only such a word as is good for edification according to the need of the moment, that it may give grace to those that hear. Ephesians 4:29

Let your speech always be with grace, seasoned, as it were, with salt so that you may know how you

should respond to each person. Colossians 4:6

This is how God says that we should be with every person. 'Let **no** unwholesome word come out of your mouth. 'Let your speech **always** be with grace. I know that this is how we often work, while we are out in company of other people. We tend to be on our best behavior. Then when we get home behind our front doors we let it all out upon whoever is closest at the time. Be it our spouse or children. We should be treating the people that are closest to us with more love and respect than we do people outside our families.

Yes, it is right to train children to have respect for other people, but you have to show that respect within your own home. Failure to do this sends wrong and mixed messages to children. That it is right to act respectful when out, or in company. That is alright also to behave in a bad and disrespectful way at home to members of the family. I am sure that this is not the lesson, training that you want your children to receive.

You want to give the best training to your children, I know this. You work at getting your children into the best schools, so that they get the best education. I tell you what, if they do not get good training at home it does not matter too much which school they go to. They can still fail, simply because of the way that they are treated at home.

The best teaching, training should come at home from parents. School will give them the way of the world's ideas and training; give them worldly views on everything. Where you can give them the best training in the way God views everything.

Let's train out children up in the way that they should go, not in the way that the worlds says is right. The worlds idea of what is right, is all about worldly success. Getting what you want, as much as you want. It is about getting money, being the best, even about being famous.

Train them up in the way that God says is right, "And they will not depart from it, even when they are old." If they then get all the money, all the success, all the notoriety, it will be all good. It will be built on the truth, and grace of God. God is not against success and all that goes with it. He is for it, so the successful will give God glory for the success that God has brought to them.

Let your light shine before men in such a way that they may see your good works, and glorify your father who is in Heaven. Matthew 5:16

This verse clearly says that we are to show the world what it is that our faith can accomplish, using God's wisdom rather than the world's. Training is a lifelong experience. We should never stop learning, but what we understand and learn the most comes from what we have already learnt as children. In a sense we become what we were taught. Like Jesus, He grew up as a carpenters son, He learned carpentry.

After He was baptised and tempted, Jesus went back to his hometown, and the people could not reconcile that Jesus was what they heard He was, because they knew Him. Jesus grew up around them. He was a carpenter, they had furniture made by Him and his brothers.

They saw Jesus as the man, that He had been trained to be a carpenter by His earthly father Joseph. Not as the Man He was in His heavenly Father. They were not there when God's voice came and said, "This is My beloved Son in whom I am well Pleased."

Even Jesus had to do works so that people saw and glorified God. We should do as Jesus did, and train our children to do as we do, as we do the works that Jesus did. I know that sounds a mouth full, but it is true, and right.

We train by example and teaching; example is probably the most dynamic and powerful form of teaching. This is because the pupils get to see a real and living, and active faith at work. They get to see the fruits of faith at work. If you walk in faith. If not, then there is no example to follow. But Jesus said:

My Father is glorified by this, that you bear much fruit, and so prove to be my disciples. John 15:8

Truly, truly, I say unto you, he who believes in Me, the works that I do, he will do also; and greater works than these he will do, because I go to the Father. John 14:12

Yes, we are to be an example in every way, in every area of our lives. Then, how we would not only impact our own children, but every child that comes into contact with our children. We are told as fathers not to provoke our children to anger. Just as we are supposed to treat everybody else in the Lord. God even tells us to bless our enemies.

So we should be treating our children even better than our enemies. All the time. How often we go about hurting the ones we love, rather than blessing them and building them up. This is not God's way.

What is God's way? Jesus came to show to us the Father. The way that God thinks and wants to deal with us. In turn He wants us to treat others in the same manner. How many times do you read of Jesus getting angry at people because of sin in their lives? He healed people and said to them, "Go and sin no more." There was no rebuking, or chastisement. Just love and forgiveness. Teaching and advice.

And fathers, do not provoke your children to anger; but bring them up in the discipline and instruction of the Lord. Ephesians 6:4

Do you want to know how to raise children in the Lord, by use of the gifts of the Spirit, and enormously by use of the Fruit of the Spirit. Just think about it. If you apply all of the qualities of the Fruit of the Spirit. There would be no room for anger in any way shape or form. Using the Fruit of the Spirit, there is no provision for sin. You know the old saying, 'that if you give a smile away, it comes back to you.' The. same is true of all aspects of the Fruit of the Spirit. That is a statement to think about as you read these verses.

But the fruit of the Spirit is, love, joy, peace, patience, kindness, goodness, faithfulness, gentleness, self-control; against such things there is no law. Galatians 5:22-23

Discipline originally the meaning was 'an instruction'. As Jesus instructed His disciples. There, right there the word, 'disciples,' Disciples were disciplined by Jesus. The word is of the same origin. Discipline is not punishment, it is teaching, training. God does not and will not punish us. God's discipline is to lead us guide us to the truth. That is one reason for the gift of the Holy Spirit, to guide us into all truth. He does this in love, not through punishment. That is why the word of God says:

Do not be conformed to this world, but be

transformed by the renewing of your mind, so that you may prove what the will of God is, that which is good and acceptable and perfect. Romans 12:2

Chapter 10: Abundant Life

I came that they might have life and have it abundantly. John 10:10

Who is Jesus talking about in this verse? The 'they' He is talking about is <u>anyone</u> who enters through Him. Anyone who becomes born again through accepting Jesus as their Saviour and has entered into eternal life. ANYONE! Every adult and child can have eternal abundant life. There are some that think that this is talking about the life to come. That great and glorious day when we get to heaven.

I can understand why people can think this. The truth is this, that the word of God is given so that we can prosper in every area of our lives right here and now, every day. In this life, that we live every day. Even in the so-called Lord's prayer Jesus said the we should command, "God's will to be done on earth as it is in heaven. "Give us this day our daily bread."

This is eternal life, that they may know You, the only true God and Jesus Christ whom You have sent. John 17:3

We have eternal life here and now in this life. If you know Jesus, and the Father. I know that it can happen that someone can become born again, accept Jesus as Lord and Saviour, and not go on to get to know the Father, and the Lord Jesus.

Jesus said so in the parable of the sower. The cares of the world choke the word of God received, or do not put down good roots, and so get scorched by the heat. These people are not walking in the eternal life that the Lord gave. The seed, which is the word of God, that fell onto good ground produced a crop of thirty, sixty, even a hundred-fold. This is an abundance. This is the eternal, abundant life that we should be walking in.

A way of thinking

If our God is a good God, a good Father, a God that loved us so much that He sent His Son Jesus. To show to us how we ought to be living; how we should be treating people. To teach to us the Father's will for us with the words of eternal life. That God would allow His Son to die in place of us, for our sins. Yes, a good, good Father, as the song goes. He set us free from the law of sin and death.

This is our God, He is awesome. If this is how good our God is? Once we have accepted Jesus as our Saviour, why would He want us to continue in sicknesses, physical or mental? Why would He want us to continue in poverty? Jesus said in the world we will have tribulation, but through His Spirit we have the power to overcome the world. Just as He has overcome the world.

For whatever is born of God overcomes the world; and this is the victory that has overcome the world – our faith. 1 John 5:4

Do you know this to be the truth. If yes, great. If no, you do not understand what the word of God says. You do not know who you are in the Lord Jesus Christ. How can we pass onto our children things that we do not understand ourselves? We have abundant life, yet most of us do not look to see; what an abundant life is; what the bible says that an abundant life is.

Too many churches seem to have spent years teaching against abundant life. Saying things like God allowed sickness, to teach us something, or poverty to keep us humble. These are lies. It is not biblical, new covenant teaching at all. We may have trials and tribulations, but they are not sent by God.

They are weapons of the devil designed to take away our faith in the Lord. Our hope of eternal life. But he cannot take it from us. Just try to make our lives miserable. That is not the life God wants for us. He has given to us eternal life, and abundant life.

Be renewed in the spirit of your mind, and put on the new self, which in the likeness of God has been created in righteousness and holiness of the truth. Ephesians 4:23-24

Abundant life is in us and should be flowing out of us. Without eternal life we cannot have the abundant life that is also a promise of God. If you are in Christ; that is if Christ is in you by the Holy Spirit, then we should also have abundant life. One of the names of God is, El Shaddai. The God of more than enough. The God of abundance.

We are to have the blessing of Abraham. Every blessing that we have is from God. They are Spiritual blessings. James tells us that every good and perfect gift comes down from the Father. Comes down to us, we do not have to wait until we get to heaven. We have every Spiritual blessing that is in heavenly places here and now on this earth.

Blessed be the God and Father of our Lord Jesus Christ, who has blessed us with every Spiritual blessing in the heavenly places in Christ. Ephesians 1:3

So, what is abundant life? It is about being prosperous. Not just in wealth, and things that come with wealth. It is not just being healthy in body and mind. It is not just having so much joy, that it just flows out of us everywhere we go. It is not just having peace in our minds and hearts, being at peace with everyone, and everything we do. It is not even being so full of God's love that everyone thinks well of us as we give out that love.

Abundant life is all of these things and more. It is about the covenant of grace that God put into place with us. It is a part of the covenant of the blood of Jesus, when He died on the cross. By His stripes we are healed. He was wounded for our transgressions. He was bruised for our iniquities. The chastisement for our peace was upon Him. This is every area of our lives almost, Mind, body and soul. Yet there is still more. This next scripture is talking about physical wealth.

Prosperity

For you know the grace of our Lord Jesus Christ, that though He was rich, yet for your sake He became poor, so that through His poverty might become rich. 2 Corinthians 8:

Jesus gave up His riches to become poor. When did Jesus become poor? It was on the cross. Poverty along with sin and sickness were all dealt with at the death of Jesus. For you and your children. There are reasons why Christians are poor. Some are to do with poor choices made in life, some are to do with the teaching they received. Some I am sure are just to do with laziness. Whatever the reason, poverty is not a part of God's plan for your life. Poverty is a curse of the law; we are redeemed from the curse of the law.

If you study the stories of Jesus you will find that He had at least one house, which was a beach front property. It was not a small house either, as the story goes that Pharisees and lawyers from every town and city in Galilee, and Judea and Jerusalem were packed into the house at one time and overflowing from the house.

So many people, that four other people with a paralysed man had to break through the roof and get access to Jesus. He had a treasurer amongst His disciples, in charge of the money. Giving to the poor. So, Jesus was not poor, if He was giving to the poor.

Jesus was wealthy why would He not be? The word also says that people were giving of their wealth to Him. Kings of the east came and gave gifts of gold. Gifts of frankincense, and gifts of myrrh, also other treasures, to Him as a young child of about two years old.

They were presenting gifts to a king, so it would have been much gold. They would not have travelled thousands of miles just to present a small gift would they? No, they Saw a star and knew that this king was special.

Jesus was rich as a child while growing up, as an adult working as a master carpenter. He must have been probably the best master carpenter around. As such it would follow that he was in great demand as a carpenter. Then when He started His ministry, people were giving much to Him. So then, it must have been on the cross that He became poor for us, that we might become rich.

This is exciting to me as I write this. Yes, the realisation that salvation, health and wealth are part of the new covenant of grace. I know that I have just written words that the Holy Spirit has put into my mind, but the scriptures are in my mind that will prove all of this. I want to show you all of what an abundant life includes. We will go through though the word and see what it actually says, that we should walk also as Jesus walked.

The blessing of Abraham

In order that in Christ Jesus the blessing of Abraham might come to the gentiles, so that we would receive the promise of the Spirit through faith. Galatians 3:14

The blessing of Abraham came before the law, and so is not under the covenant of the law. God blessed Abraham in that he became very wealthy. Kings came to him to make a pact to protect themselves, thinking that Abraham might attack them and take away their kingdoms.

God's word says that we are to have the blessing of Abraham. The blessing was not just to be the father of many nations. That we are his descendants, through faith in Christ. The blessing of Abraham was to inherit the land, to become prosperous in every way. If we become rich though, it is for a purpose. God's purpose.

When Abraham sent his servant to his relatives to find a wife for Isaac. The servant said to them, that God had greatly blessed Abraham, with many flocks, herds, with gold and silver and many riches. That as he said was how God had blessed Abraham. That is the blessing of Abraham. That passed on to his descendants, even Ismael got blessed because of the promise of God to Abraham.

The rest of the blessing of Abraham was to him a matter of his faith. A promise for the future. In the meantime, God blessed him in the here and now. Possibly as the wealthiest person on the face of the earth at that time.

And God is able to make all grace abound to you, so that always having all sufficiency in everything, you may have an abundance for every good deed. 2 Corinthians 9:8

God's promises say that we will have more than enough. In every area of our lives. 'For every good deed'. During the discourse of Jesus where He came to the above verse about abundant life. He makes a reference to an old testament scripture about the blessing of keeping the law. Where Moses wrote about the blessings and the curses associated with keeping or braking the law.

Before we look at that I need to point out that we are not under law, but under grace. As it says many times in the new testament. The reason for this is Jesus. He redeemed us from the curse of the law. Abraham had a better covenant than the law. The Bible says that we have a better covenant than the law.

Christ redeemed us from the curse of the law, having become a curse for us, for it is written, "cursed is everyone who hangs on a tree. Galatians 3:13

We cannot fulfil the law, but Jesus did, on our behalf. He took away all the curses of the law that are written and bore them in His body. This is so we did not have to accept any of the curses that try to come upon us. Sicknesses and diseases, aches and pains, even poverty is a curse of the law. We should be enjoying the blessings of God, not the curses of the law. So, the thing that Jesus said, that relates back to the blessings of obeying the law. The one thing I want to point out, is this underlined:

I am the door; if anyone enters through Me, he will be saved, <u>and will go in and out and find pasture.</u> John 10:9

and back in Deuteronomy 28, it says this:

Blessed will you be in the city, blessed will you be in the field. Blessed shall you be when you come in, blessed will you be when you go out. Deuteronomy 28:3,5

Blessings everywhere! When do we have eternal life? We have it now; we are living in eternal life now. We should be living in abundant life now also. The simple answer to what is abundant life, is to be living each and every day in all of the blessings of God.

That is spiritually, physically, and financially. God is concerned with every area of our lives. The blessings in Deuteronomy include blessings of the fruit of our bodies, (children). Blessings on the fruit of our labors, (financial). Blessings on our storehouses, (savings). It says that He will establish us as a holy nation, (Spiritually).

For you are a Chosen race, a royal priesthood, a holy nation, a people for God's own possession, so that you may proclaim the excellencies of Him, who has called you out of darkness into His marvelous light. 1 Peter 2:9

Health

This is how God sees us. This is a part of abundant life, to show, proclaim, to share the excellencies of Him who called us. We do this by the way we live abundantly, and tell with words and actions how we are blessed by God.

In the place that I work as far as I know I am the only employee that does not have time off work for sickness. I was actually told this by my department boss about three years ago, whether I am the only one, now I am not sure. It is noticed by my employers.

When they mention something about it to me, it is an opportunity for me to share my faith. The reasons for my walking/living in divine health. I even get to give testimonies of how, if I began to feel the symptoms of illness and had to rebuke them and stay healthy. This is a part of living an abundant life, walking by the Spirit.

Knowing that I, we have the power to be in control of anything that comes against us. This is true in every part of our lives, spiritually, physically and financially. It is a walk of faith. We should be walking in the demonstration of the power of God every day.

The kingdom of God is within us. God is within us through the power of the Holy Spirit. We are a part of the house of God. God says in 1 Peter that, 'We are Living stones.' That means we are not dead; we are alive in Him. Jesus is alive in us. That life of Jesus should be flowing out of us, through us. To our children and to everyone we meet. We have the same power and authority that was with Jesus, because He is in us. By His Spirit, we can do all things through Christ who strengthens us.

All things mean's all things. Abundant life, where nothing will be able to stand against us. God is for us. Do you believe the word of God. Man shall not live by bread alone, but by every word that proceeds from the mouth of God. If we are to walk in the same manner as Jesus walked, that includes in divine health. This comes through the word. Jesus is The word. The Word is in us, alive and active.

Incline your ears to My words, "For they are life to those who find them and health to all their Body". Proverbs 4;22

If you attend to the word of God; receive it and live it, you should not get sick, you will have health to all your body. We are made in the image of God. Spirit and soul clothed in a body. Three in one. You could say that we are a holy trinity. Just as God is, Father, Son and Holy Spirit. We have the Holy Spirit living inside of us.

We are holy because He is holy. Some come to God in an attitude of unworthiness. This should not be if you read and understand all of the benefits of the new life that we have in Christ. We should read and search the word for the great things God says and has done for us. We need to get to know exactly who we are in Christ.

Do you not know that you are a temple of God, and that the Spirit of God dwells in you? If any man destroys the temple of God, God will destroy him, for the temple of God is holy, and that is what you are. 1 Corinthians 3:16-17

We are the Holy temple of God. Once we know who we are in Christ, we can begin to understand the truth of all the blessings that God has laid up for us. Not for when we get to heaven, but for right here and now in this life, on this earth. Our sins are forgiven now. Not only ours but those of the whole world. We have eternal life now; and so can every person in the whole world.

By his stripes we are healed now! It is the truth, just as we have salvation now; we also have healing. It is not just talking about spiritual healing; this was done when we accepted Jesus as our Saviour. It is talking about physical healing. This was all accomplished on the cross. Jesus bore our sicknesses. He received our sin and sickness into His body.

Curses and blessings

Because of sin god introduced the law. It is a covenant with God. There are blessings for obeying the law, and curses for disobeying. We have already seen that Jesus has redeemed us from the curse of the law. Let's look at what is the curse of the law.

What happens when we live according to the law, and not fulfil the law. The agreement/covenant of the law is broken. I am not going to write out the bulk of Deuteronomy 28, but just give a summary.

You will be cursed in the city, and the country. Your children shall be cursed. The land will be cursed, the produce of the ground. You will have a curses of, confusion and rebuke in all that you try to do. Pestilence, fever, consumption, inflammation and fiery heat and mildew. Your enemies will defeat you (our enemies are the devil and his demons). Boils, and tumors, scabs and itching, madness and blindness and bewilderment of heart.

You will not prosper in your ways. Adultery will be rife; this includes divorce. You will be oppressed and depressed. You will borrow money but not be a lender. You will become poor as your businesses fail. (Poverty).

Hostilities within the family. Severe and lasting plagues, and chronic illnesses. Any sickness/disease not written in this book.

This is an impressive list of the curses of the law, and there is more. How many of these things can you identify with that are prevalent in our societies today? Even within Christian circles. Jesus has set us free from the curse of the law. We still have free will and as such we can open ourselves up to some of these things. How you may ask?

Our spirits are saved and sealed by the Holy Spirit. Our bodies are still temporary flesh. They will be made immortal when we meet Jesus. Our minds are in the process of being saved. They are or should be, being renewed. That is why God says:

Do not be conformed to this world, but be transformed by the renewing of your mind, that you may prove what the will of God is, that which is good, acceptable and perfect. Romans 12:2

How do we find the will of God? The answer to that is easy, we read the word of God. The word of god is truth. You will know the truth and the truth will set you free. Once you are free, then you can begin to live the abundant life that God has planned for you. The truth is the whole of the gospel.

Not just salvation, it also includes health to our bodies and minds; and the blessing of the work of our hands to prosper us. The word says whatever you do, do it as unto the Lord. If we do that, then the Lord will prosper it. There are plenty of times from the mouth of Jesus, that He says that God will give what you ask of Him. There are a couple of criteria, ask according to God's will and ask in faith, without doubting.

For everyone who asks receives, and to him who seeks finds, and to him who knocks finds........ If you then being evil know how to give good gifts to your children, how much more will your Father who is in heaven give what is good to those who ask Him. Matthew 7;8,11

So, now let's look and see what the blessing of obeying the law are. They are all of the blessings that were promised to Abraham, right down to the blessing of offspring. It says that all of these blessings will come upon you and overtake you. Which kind of means there will be so much you may not know what to do with it.

You will be blessed in the city and blessed in the country. Blessed shall be the offspring of your body and that of your animals, the produce of your ground. Your food will be blessed. You will be blessed when you come in and when you go out. Your enemies will be defeated. Your savings will be blessed and all the work of your hands. You will abound in prosperity, and in all the things above. You will lend and not have to borrow. The Lord will make you the head and not the tail. Why will God do all this? So that people will see that you are the children of God. It is for His purpose that He will give you a life of abundance.

Here is the truth, the thing that so many of us do not realise or understand. We are righteous, Jesus fulfilled the law for us, on our behalf. He made us righteous in the sight of God. God no longer looks down upon us as a people stained by sin. He has removed our sin from us. Washed us clean by the blood of Jesus. He sees no sin that can get in the way of His blessing us.

The only things that can get in the way is our unbelief. Our choice not to believe Him, not to have faith in Him. Not to trust Him and His promises. Not to trust in Him is actually the same sin that caused the fall of Adam and Eve. Satan caused them to doubt the word of God. Abundant life comes through trusting God and His word.

Demonstration of our faith comes through the out working of our faith. We are not saved by works, but we cannot operate in faith without works. Now, when we start talking about works, I am sure, that a lot of Christians will start thinking along the lines of a specific work for the ministry, or work for God that the people do.

Yes, it can mean this, but also it is about living according to God's plan for our lives: in each and every little thing that we have to do. If we walk by faith, it will show up in the way we go about our normal everyday lives. Making choices and in everything we say and do.

Whatever you do in word or deed, do all in the name of the Lord Jesus, giving thanks through Him to God the Father. Colossians 3:17

Living an abundant life is a choice. We can choose to live the worlds way, according to the way the world says to do things. Or we can choose to live according to God's word, doing things God's way. Which do you think will be of more benefit, or profitable to you. Remember the blessings from Deuteronomy 28. I want to live God's way and an abundant way. A Life full to overflowing with God's blessings. We all should desire this.

That is the desire of God for us. So, when Jesus said that God will give you the desires of your heart, this what it means. When you desire for yourself what God desires for you, you will get it when you ask Him. This is living the abundant life that God wants us to live.

Demonstration

We should be living a life that is a good example to our children of how to live and walk by faith. Children learn more by example than being told. That is why as swimming teachers we are told to give good and correct demonstration of how we want swimmers to use their arms and legs.

If we demonstrate the right way of living, our children will copy. If we demonstrate the wrong way to be living, guess what? Our children will copy. Even if you tell them the right thing, they will copy your example. This is true, and so, if we live a life demonstrating abundant life, our children will want to copy, especially as they see the fruits of that life.

And my message and my preaching were not in persuasive words of wisdom, but in demonstration of the Spirit and of power, so that your faith would not rest on the wisdom of men, but on the power of God. 1 Corinthians 2:4-5

This may seem a slightly strange scripture to apply here. What it is saying is two things that I want to point out. Firstly, speaking God's word does not have to be complicated with great words of wisdom. It just simply has to be the truth. This is the same when sharing God's word with children.

If you seek you will find. If you ask you will receive. If you knock on God's door He will open it for you.

Secondly, the truth has to be demonstrated. You cannot demonstrate the power of the Spirit, if you don't have the baptism in the Spirit. Demonstration of the power of God's word followed the Apostles preaching.

This then is a truth we need to understand, that if we say one thing then do something different, we are lying. Either we are lying with our words, or we are lying in the demonstration of our lives. A child sees the difference and is more likely to follow the demonstration. Because the words say something contrary, they will forget the words, and do as you do.

If you live according to the word of God, they will copy you. If you demonstrate a life that is full of the power of the Holy Spirit, they will want the same life. If you demonstrate a life that is full of god's abundant blessing, your children will want to live that way too.

In the same way, the demonstration of the power of God should accompany the speaking the word of God. This ought to be happening in our daily lives, with our children witnessing the power of living an abundant life.

That is how the early church grew. That should be how the church should have been growing through the last two thousand plus years. If the church is not growing then something must be missing? The demonstration of the power of god's word. It should start where we are, at home in the family. With our children, not excluding them. Then it will spread out into our communities.

If we live and walk in faith, it becomes contagious. It will infect, affect and effect every area of our lives. People will see it and be drawn to the Lord. Our children will see it and not want to live any other way. We should not be having our young people saying things like, "before I settle down and make commitments I want to travel and see the world a bit."

That is like saying that I want to see what the world has to offer before I make a commitment to live my life. The world has nothing to offer anyone, compared to what God has to offer. What God has planned for their lives.

They don't see God's blessings upon the lives of their parents, or many of the significant adults in their lives; in or out of church. So they want to go see if they can find themselves out there in the world. When all that they need is within them. If they have been born again and filled with the Holy Spirit. If they see and experience an abundant life why would they want to go out and seek second best?

Train up a child in the way he should go, even when he is old he will not depart from it. Proverbs 22:6

Are we the blind leading the blind?

As we have seen we cannot teach what we do not know. We cannot teach what we do not practice. Training up a child is passing on not only information, it is demonstration of life. If the only time your children see you praying is when you are putting them to bed, they will learn that bedtime is the only time to pray. Which we know is a lie.

If the only time that your children see you pray is when you are at church, this cannot be right. We are not living a Christian life as an example to them. On the other hand if we pray at any time about everything, they will learn that they can pray at any time.

From the day they are born we should be praying and worshipping God in the presence of our children. Yes you can have a time in devotion apart from them, but if you want them to follow in your footsteps as far as your Christian life and devotion to God is concerned, you have to include them in your life with God.

They have to learn and understand that; your God is their God also. That God is as interested in their lives as He is in yours. If they see that you have a living and active relationship with your Heavenly Father, they will want that also.

If we are living our Christian life in the way that the world thinks it should be, or our own interpretation We may well be missing the truth. Children are a part of the church of today. If you only consider them to be the church of the future, and teach them wrong, what sort of church will that future church be. Maybe a lot worse than some churches are today. Following practices and wrong doctrines.

Training is not just speaking and telling children how they should be. Not just telling them the right way to go. God confirms His word by demonstration of power. Our lives should be the same, having God confirm our words by demonstration of power. Training is more showing the way to go, than telling. It is an everyday demonstration of the Christian life.

Acknowledgments

There have been many inspirations that have gone towards writing this book. The children, many hundreds of them, that I have had the pleasure of working with. Both within the Christian world and in the secular world also. Of course, this includes my own two children, Dawn and Benjamin.

I have to thank all of the Preachers, teachers, and pastors that have had influence over me and fed to me the incorruptible word of God, throughout my Christian life. Firstly, a pastor and dear brother in Christ, Mans Yousuf. Then people that I have listened to for about five years to date, that have helped me to understand who we are in Christ. Americans Tony Evans and John Gray who God used to relight the fire of the Holy Spirit within me.

Many thanks to Andrew Womack and the teachings of his ministry, that confirmed so many things that I already knew deep in my heart. Brought them to the surface, to help me to stand on the truth of God's word.

And above all, thanks be to the God and Father of our Lord Jesus Christ, who has blessed us with every Spiritual blessing that is in Heavenly places in Christ.

About the Author

Charles King was born in Leicester UK in 1958, as Wayne King. He was given up for adoption from birth. When adopted was given the middle name of Charles, and the adopted surname of Humphries. In the mid 1970's began using Charlie as his main name. About 1990 he changed his name back to his birth name of King, after the death of both of his adopted parents.

In 2008, he was reunited with his birth mother, who was living the USA at the time. It was a very good reunion and the relationship continues in a good way. He has two adult children, Dawn and Benjamin and two grandchildren to Dawn, Dakota and Arlo. There is an extended family by marriage, with three adult children and a grandchild, Conan.

Charlie King has spent the last 40 years working with children in local churches. Also, as part of his employment working as a swimming teacher and a diving coach, in the UK. He became and has been a swimming teacher since 1981. Then a diving coach since 2008 and has had influence upon hundreds of children for good. Both to the gospel and in his work teaching much needed life skills. Both as a coach and swimming teacher; and a teacher of God's word.

This book represents the heart of a man, that has the desires of God towards children and the right way to train children up in the things of God. Knowing that everything that God has given to him and indeed any adult; the gifts, the talents, are for all who call upon the name of the Lord. It does not matter how old, we can all be used of God. That we should be developing the gifts and talents that are already within our children, placed there by God.

46897231R00122

Printed in Poland
by Amazon Fulfillment
Poland Sp. z o.o., Wrocław